The World of..
English

428 HEA

D0532786

LEARNING. services

Falmouth Marine School
Learning Centre

01326 310319

This resource is to be returned on or before the last date stamped below. To renew items please contact the Centre

Three Week Loan

Alison Head

FA005574

CORNWALL COLLEGE

Contents

Page

4–5	Make your mind up...	Writing to argue
6–7	Oh, go on then...	Writing to persuade
8–9	I wouldn't do that if I were you...	Writing to advise
10–11	Here's why!	Writing to inform
12–13	I'll give you several good reasons...	Writing to explain
14–15	Tell me more!	Writing to describe
16–17	Oh, use your imagination...	Writing to explore/imagine entertain
18–19	What did you think?	Writing to analyse/review/comment
20–21	Brainstorm	Writing types
22–23	Test your knowledge 1	
24–25	I want to tell you a story...	Prose
26–27	Poetry in motion	Poetry
28–29	Exit stage left	Drama/Shakespeare
30–31	He seems a bit dodgy to me...	Character
32–33	What an atmosphere!	Atmosphere/Mood/Setting
34–35	Security blanket	Language – techniques used by writers
36–37	Are you posh?	Language – formal usage and its effects
38–39	No, I'm common!	Language – informal usage and its effects
40–41	Brainstorm	Fiction text types
42–43	Test your knowledge 2	

44–45	Do you need a break?	**Information texts**
46–47	Life of a legend	**Recount texts**
48–49	Are you following this?	**Explanation texts**
50–51	Don't panic!	**Instructions**
52–53	Try and make me…	**Persuasion**
54–55	Say what you really think…	**Reviews**
56–57	This is what we think…	**Editorial/opinion texts**
58–59	It's not really an uphill struggle!	**Description**
60–61	Brainstorm	**Non-fiction text types**
62–63	Test your knowledge 3	
64–65	Mnemonics might be necessary	**Spelling 1**
66–67	Spelling rules, OK!	**Spelling 2**
68–69	Spot the full stop	**Punctuation**
70–71	Stay on topic!	**Paragraphs**
72–73	Super structure	**Structure**
74–75	Variety is the spice of life	**Sentence variety**
76–77	It depends where you're standing	**The writer's viewpoint**
78–79	Seeing red	**Common errors to avoid**
80–81	How to revise	**Ways of making revision better!**
82–89	Practice paper	
90	Glossary	
91–96	Answers	

Make your mind up...

How would you like it if you were made to stay on at school until you were 19? That is exactly the issue I want to discuss in the next lines.

Firstly, I feel that, with five per cent of pupils leaving school with few or no qualifications, it would be a positive step. Why? Well, because it would give them extra time to achieve something and would provide the country with a better-educated workforce.

I think that one good reason to raise the school leaving age would be to keep young people off the unemployment figures. Unemployment today stands at around two million people.

Three hundred thousand of the unemployed are between 16 and 19. If we kept them in education, and the money that would otherwise be spent on paying out benefits could be used to provide them with more education and training, when they did enter the workforce, they would be better equipped. Opponents of this view might say that they might not need this training, but what evidence do they have to offer?

In opposition to this, however, some would say that keeping pupils forcibly in education until the age of 19 would be a bad move. There would almost certainly be civil disobedience, and where would the education officers and social workers come from to enforce this new legislation?

Overall, based on just these brief responses, I personally feel that staying on at school until 19 would be a bad idea. Despite the benefits that it might bring, the actual and social costs, as I have mentioned, would be far too high.

Each new point is in a new paragraph

Varied paragraph openings

Rhetorical question

Alternative viewpoint

Conclusion reflects the ideas discussed

THIS AFFECTS YOU!

Argumentative writing

Hardly a detailed argument, is it? However, it carries many of the features of **argumentative writing** that you will need to use in your SATs.

Argumentative writing is the type in which you will be expected to discuss both sides of a controversial topic and draw your own conclusions at the end. It might be part of a persuasive piece of writing too, or it might just be an argument for its own sake.

Oh no it isn't.

Oh yes it is.

EXAMINER'S TOP TIPS

The links between your paragraphs are an important style feature in argumentative writing. Don't start paragraphs with 'My first point is', 'My second point is'. To reach higher levels, vary your paragraph openers by using phrases like 'A further issue is...', 'In addition to this I feel...'.

Balance doesn't mean the same number of points on both sides - it simply means that you consider views from both sides.

Your conclusion should reflect and be based on the arguments you have used in the main part of your essay.

KEY FACTS

1 **Make sure you have ideas for:**

   ⬆ **the introduction**
   ➡ **both viewpoints**
   ⬇ **the conclusion**

2 **Each new point should be in a new paragraph.**

3 **Remember to vary paragraph openings.**

4 **Remember to look at the alternative viewpoint.**

5 **Use <u>rhetorical questions</u>, statistics and detailed comments.**

6 **Make sure your conclusion reflects the ideas you have discussed**

Oh, go on then...

I'm talking to you personally, because I know that you are such a sweet, intelligent, good-natured and – dare I say it – good-looking person. I am just a poor, underpaid worker, who nobody cares about. It would be nice to be noticed by someone for a change and especially by someone as clever as you.

Haven't you ever been refused money? Haven't you ever been treated this way? We have all experienced the problem of not having enough cash in our lives and have longed achingly for someone to get rid of our terrible, unfair, hideous burden of poverty. Having said that, I'm the only one who's suffering this badly at the moment.

That's why I'm asking you for a loan. I'm not asking you because I'm trying to take advantage of you. I'm not asking you because I know you're kind-hearted. I'm asking you because I know that you are the kind of person who likes to do a stranger a favour.

Miss M T Pockets

PS If you don't lend me the money, I'll send the boys round...

Labels:
- Personal address
- Flattery
- Rhetorical question
- Get the audience on your side
- Emotive language
- Make the reader feel guilty
- Three-part repetition
- Threat

Persuasive writing

Did that work? Are you going to give her the money? Maybe you were slightly swayed. Perhaps you felt sorry for her. If you did, it's because she used techniques of **persuasive writing**.

Persuasive writing is one of the writing types that you may come across in your SATs and can take many forms. You might be writing a begging letter, appealing to people to donate to charity or asking your parents to increase your pocket money! It won't matter what you are trying to get someone to do, but it will matter how you try to persuade them. For that reason it's important to know a few persuasive tricks... you might even use them to get a pocket money increase too!

EXAMINER'S TOP TIPS

You don't need to use every technique listed here in every piece of persuasive writing. Choose the ones that suit your needs and your audience.

In general, it's good to start with flattery and end with three-part repetition, because flattery puts the reader in a good mood and the three-part repetition leaves your reader with the most important issues firmly in their mind.

Try thinking of examples of persuasive writing in both formal and informal situations. Informal - persuading a friend/family member. Formal - persuading an authority figure/teacher/politician.

KEY FACTS

☑ **Personal address.** Address your audience personally – use 'you'.

☑ **Get the audience on your side.** Use the word 'we' as it makes your audience feel as though you, the writer, and they, the reader, are working together to achieve a common goal.

☑ **Rhetorical questions.** When you use one of these, you don't have to give the answer – it is suggested, and so you try to manipulate the way the reader thinks.

☑ **Emotive language.** This is often used to make the reader feel sympathy for someone or something. Be careful not to overuse it because it can have the opposite effect and put people off.

☑ **Odd one out/making someone feel guilty.** This can sometimes be combined with emotive language, but it can also be used as a separate technique. It's another way of making the reader sympathetic to the writer's viewpoint.

☑ **Threats/Blackmail.** This may not always work, but in some circumstances – where the writer is desperate – it might. Be careful not to use silly threats, as they will have the opposite effect to the one you wanted.

☑ **Flattery.** There's no better way to get someone on your side than by being nice to them. Again, don't go over the top or it will have the opposite effect.

☑ **Three-part repetition.** This is often a good, memorable way to end your persuasive piece, as it's a catchy and simple way of coming up with something that your readers will remember.

I wouldn't do that if I were you...

Picture the scene. You are sitting in your bedroom. No one is chatting on the internet on your Instant Messenger Program. You have a pile of homework the size of a small European mountain range. There's nothing on TV.

You decide to tidy your room.

Hold it *right* there!

Let me give you some advice...

Reasons why you should not tidy your bedroom

What follows will give you some reasons why you should not attempt to do such a foolish thing without fully considering the consequences. ———

> Purpose stated in opening

1 It will give your parents no reason to communicate with you.
2 You might find something that you'd rather not, like more homework or your little brother's three-week-old pizza slice.
3 You won't be able to find anything.
4 Your friends will wonder what is up with you.

> Numbered points

Should you wish to ignore this advice, then be aware that there might be several consequences. Your parents might be unaccountably pleasant to you. Your teachers may also momentarily get off your back, especially if you give in the homework that you've rediscovered – if you did it in the first place, that is. Most importantly, you will probably find that your bedroom actually has a floor and, quite possibly, a carpet.

> Conditional phrase

> Modal verbs

Overall, my advice would be only to tidy your bedroom in extreme circumstances, as it could cause you unnecessary trouble and suffering. ———

> Conclusion

Advice writing

This is an example of **advice writing**. If you are giving advice, you need to phrase your ideas very carefully. Think about the consequences of wrongly taken advice, whether helping a friend with an emotional problem, or helping someone to wire a plug.

Remember that there is a fine line between advice and instruction. Advice is not as definite as instruction, so make sure you look closely at what the task you've been set is asking you to do. It may require you to phrase your ideas quite differently. If you want to get Level 5 or above in your SATs, you'll need to know the differences.

EXAMINER'S TOP TIPS

Think about who you are giving advice to - that will affect whether you use a formal or an informal style. Both are possible with advice writing.

Decide whether bullet points are appropriate - with a problem page advice text you might not use them, but with other kinds of advice writing, such as exam advice, it is fine!

Make a plan of what is going to go at the start, in the middle and at the end.

KEY FACTS

Remember to include:

1 an **opening**, in which you state your purpose – what are you giving advice about?

2 **bullet points or numbering** – these help to make your main pieces of advice clearer

3 a section where you **develop your basic advice** and look at the outcomes or consequences of the advice

4 <u>modal verbs</u> and <u>conditional</u> phrases – you might not be definite about the advice you want to give, so you must phrase your ideas carefully. Notice how it says 'you **could...**' not 'you **will...**'

5 a **conclusion**, in which you sum up your advice and the reasons for it.

Here's why!

Scientists have recently made startling discoveries about the relationship between tidiness and creativity. Research done by the University of Fegg Hayes shows that the more untidy you are, the greater chance you have of being a rock star, top-selling author or movie star – an 85% chance, in fact.

Contrary to popularly held beliefs put forward on TV home improvement programmes about de-cluttering your life, this research shows that the more you create a mess around yourself, the more creative you seem to be.

People who crave order tend to be mathematical or scientific thinkers – they have a need for logic and sequence. Their behaviour reveals itself in their homes, in that they fold the ends of the toilet paper, place knives and forks in separate compartments in the kitchen drawers and iron creases in the fronts of their trousers.

Creative thinkers, however, are always looking for less logical ways through life. One of the study's participants, Tara Womer of Illinois, a successful author, stated that she never tidied her house, because by leaving things around she was able to find things by going through the layers – she found things by remembering not *where* she'd put it, but *when* – if it had been bought in the last month, it was probably on show, but if it had been bought last year, it was probably six inches below the surface of her magazines and cat food.

This sort of strange logic is common among our brightest and most creative minds. So, if you are accused of being untidy, then it might be worth taking a look at this published research – if you can find where you put it.

Introduces the subject of the information

Technical language

Name

Fact

Statistic

Formal tone

Information writing

One of the main purposes of **information writing** is to present facts in a useful way. Your audience might be the readers of a guidebook, someone looking in a brochure, or a student doing research for a project. You'll need to be able to present your ideas in a clear, useful way.

In the SATs, this is a common writing type used in tasks in both the long and short answer writing questions. To achieve Level 5 or above, you will need to be clear, clean and organised. This is what the examiner will be looking for to score marks for <u>composition</u> <u>and</u> <u>effect</u>.

EXAMINER'S TOP TIPS

Plan what information you are going to put in your paragraphs. Make a list with one point per paragraph.

Use facts from your own experience if there aren't any in the stimulus material provided with the exam paper.

If you don't know any statistics, you could write down some approximate numbers. You are being tested on your knowledge of the writing style, not on whether 46% or 47% of children fall asleep in front of the computer while doing their maths homework. If you have used reasonable sounding statistics, the examiner will appreciate and understand what you are doing and you will get credit.

Avoid slang - information texts are read by a wide audience. You need to be formal so the widest possible audience can understand what you have written.

KEY FACTS

1 **The introduction gives a general idea of what kind of information is going to be delivered.**

2 **The writing includes facts, names and statistics.**

3 **Each paragraph contains different information.**

4 **The <u>tone</u> is formal.**

5 **The language may be technical if the information is about a 'specialist' subject.**

I'll give you several good reasons...

TOP SECRET

If you want to know how to succeed in your SATs, you are reading the correct part of this book. That is because the next few paragraphs are going to explain the appropriate procedures for getting in the examiner's good books.

> Introduction states the purpose

Firstly, you need to make sure you write clearly. This is because the examiner is probably really old and has bad eyesight and therefore won't be able to read small scrawny writing. If he or she (the examiner) is not able to read what you have written, you might not be given the benefit of the doubt. They might think you are writing badly because you can't spell and you are just trying to hide the fact.

> Short sentence to introduce the point

> Point backed up with a reason

Another way in which people have tried – and failed – to get on the marker's good side, is by adding a personal note at the end of their script about how they have had an endless succession of supply teachers since Year 3 and therefore they deserve a break. This doesn't work because, as most of the markers are or were teachers, they know that this is probably a lie. The marker also doesn't mark anything that is not relevant to the question, so such words have to be ignored anyway. Therefore, just stick to the task.

> Signals of explanation

> Rhetorical question

Finally, what about the urban legends of people putting money in with their SATs papers? Wouldn't that work? Well, no – chances are that it would fall out, your teacher would discover it first before the papers were sent off, or nobody would find it. If they did, you would get in serious trouble so it wouldn't be worth it.

As a result of all these things, you should just do what the SATs papers require, because time wasted thinking of not very clever ways to beat the system is time that should be spent on revising skills and techniques!

Top secret advice – no cheque book necessary

Writing to explain

Explanation is all about the quality of the reasons you give and the way you organise them. There are several writing types that explanation is linked with – information and description are two examples.

In your SATs, explanation in your writing is important, because if you don't let the marker know – in writing – **how** you have worked out your ideas, how can they give you any marks?

EXAMINER'S TOP TIPS

When you plan, make a list of each point that you wish to explain and think of at least one reason for each point. If you can think of more for some of your points, that will help you to move towards Levels 6 and 7.

Be careful with the lengths of sentences. You will need some complex sentences if you have a very complicated explanation, but don't try to fit it all into one sentence. Take it one step at a time, so that you - and your audience - know what your reasons are.

Explanation writing sometimes needs to be chronological if you have to explain things in the order in which they happen. Watch out for occasions where that may be the case.

KEY FACTS

1 Your introduction should state the purpose of your writing – what are you trying to explain?

2 Every point needs to be backed up with at least one reason.

3 Words like 'so', 'because', 'therefore' and 'consequently' and phrases such as 'as a result' are signals that you are explaining.

4 You could use rhetorical questions to raise a question that doesn't require an answer.

5 To introduce a point, use short sentences that contain just a main clause. The explanation sentences that follow should have at least a <u>main clause</u> and one <u>subordinate clause</u> in which you give your reason. If there is a variety of reasons, you will need complex sentences containing a number of additional clauses.

Tell me more!

Your bag

The bag had been left carelessly by the desk. Its creased, battered exterior suggested years of misuse and abuse. It had survived day after day of pummelling on the school bus, and wore its scars with pride – a scratch here, an oil or ink stain there and its seams were starting to fray and darken with growing grime.

Once there had been a name tag, but like an old birthday card discarded once it was past its date, it had long since disappeared. In its place there was marker pen scrawl, but mixed in among the juvenile love/hate graffiti and the latest band names, it was barely noticeable. The ripped, ragged edges of text books peeked out from under one of its flaps and screamed to be released like imprisoned souls from the stifling, never-cleaned interior.

| Adverb |
| Adjectives |
| Personification |
| Alliteration |
| Similes |

My bag

Bags should be smart, practical and useful. They should be chosen to complement the school uniform, so should therefore be a smart shade of blue, which gives off the impression of uniformity and efficiency.

Bags should be practical and of a manageable size. Big, bulky bags with several pockets are often useful for sporting activity, but inefficient, awkward and an inconsiderate obstacle in a crowded classroom. Large, shiny, synthetic fabric bags may win points in the need for social acceptance, but they will soon become worn and tatty and create an impression of untidiness and carelessness.

| Adjectives |
| Alliteration |

Writing to describe

Both of these passages are examples of **writing to describe**. You might write to describe to entertain someone, as in a story, or you might be describing something as part of an information text, to supply more detail. Depending on your viewpoint, you may need to describe things in different ways, as the two passages above show.

EXAMINER'S TOP TIPS

1 Decide what sort of description the task requires - if you are describing to entertain, it's likely that you will use a wider range of techniques than if you are describing to inform.

2 Try to use unusual examples of similes and metaphors. Simply using these techniques will probably get you towards Level 5, but if you wish to go higher, you need to show a bit more originality. Include a couple of adjectives in your similes to turn clichéd expressions into more original ones. For example, instead of saying 'As cold as ice', try 'As cold as glassy, frost-covered ice'.

3 When you plan, make a list of things about whatever you are describing - don't describe everything. Choose just to describe those things that reveal something of the character of whatever it is you are describing.

4 If you can, don't use just your eyes to describe - use your senses and describe what you can smell, touch, taste and hear, where possible.

KEY FACTS

◄ You can write to describe in different ways. The first passage is writing descriptively to entertain. The second passage is writing descriptively to inform. Despite this, they share many characteristics.

► When describing to entertain, you might use figures of speech like similes, metaphors (including personification), adjectives, adverbs and alliteration.

◄ When describing to inform, you would tend to use more adjectives than the other features mentioned.

↑ Include opinions, thoughts and feelings.

◄ Sentence types are varied to add emphasis to the words, phrases and descriptive techniques used. For example, a simile might be used at the start of a sentence for impact.

Oh, use your imagination...

There it stood, in the dim, half-lit shade of the window ... its pages were yellowed and fraying with age, like dried skin from some long forgotten beast. Above the book, tiny dust-mites hovered and floated through the bright shafts of sunlight that dared enter the sorcerer's inner sanctum. A miniscule pocket of air collected itself and ruffled the corner of the topmost pages.

The huge, lead-embossed door groaned and slowly creaked open, causing the pages to raise themselves and sink again, exhausted by the effort.

'Where on earth did I put it?' muttered the grey-bearded and wizened figure that entered the room with a faltering scuttle. The sound of bottles being raised and the smell of musty disturbance filled the room. The flailing cloth of the man's cloak scythed through the air, as he searched with an urgent desperation for the object of his quest.

With one quick turn, a click of the heels and a swift spin he was gone and the intimidating door settled once more to its close. The dusty air in the room resumed its silent vigil over the leather bound book that lay open across the ancient, worn, wooden table. Hidden from prying human eyes, something in the room exhaled. It exhaled deeply, as one who had been disturbed from sleep would. The exhaled breath tasted of age, of death and the rancid stench of fear. It was the first reluctant breath that it had taken since time immemorial...

Attention grabbing opening

Verbs create atmosphere

Descriptive vocabulary creates mood

Sense of mystery in the conclusion

So... what happens next, Dad?

That's the effect this piece of writing is supposed to have. If you are **writing to explore, imagine and entertain**, you want to get the reader's attention and then get them wanting more, while keeping their interest. Think of how much power it gives you if you can control what someone is thinking or feeling. That's what you're doing with this type of writing. The better you can do that, the more credit you will get for **composition and effect** in the SATs exam.

Exciting content is not exciting unless you **make** it exciting through description. It is far better to have a piece of writing in which very little happens, which is beautifully described, than a piece full of events with no description.

Plan what vocabulary you are going to use. Make lists, spider diagrams or mind maps by theme, such as lists of mysterious words, depending on the mood you want to create. You might also number the words by paragraph, so all the words you intend to use in paragraph one would be numbered '1'.

EXAMINER'S TOP TIPS

Try to use a range of vocabulary – when you read, build up a log of 'new' words you come across and give yourself the target of using at least one word a week in lessons at school, either in writing or orally. The more you do this, the more your vocabulary will develop and you will be able to achieve above Level 5, where a wider range of vocabulary is needed.

KEY FACTS

◄ You need an **attention-grabbing opening and conclusion**, as these are the most important parts of your structure. Here, the opening achieves this by creating a sense of mystery, as does the conclusion. By not giving things away, you have to focus on details for clues, so you read more closely.

► Use **descriptive vocabulary** that helps to create a mood or atmosphere. Note the words in this passage that are of a similar tone – they are to do with age or danger. They help to build a sinister tone by using them frequently throughout the passage.

↓ Your **choice of verbs** helps to create atmosphere – people often neglect verbs when creating a mood, but they can make a great impact when creating characters.

↑ Use **similes, metaphors, alliteration** and <u>onomatopoeia</u>. See the section on 'writing to describe' for more detail.

What did you think?

Film of the week

Yesterday, I had the misfortune of watching the most dreadful film I have ever seen. Entitled *How to lose a cat in 24 days*, it was a semi-documentary about an old lady, played by Texan actress Kelli King, whose main claim to fame was the fact that she kept losing her pets. That was the basis of the plot, but there was also a subplot concerning the lady's relationship with neighbour Mr Duvi (David Shaw).

Supposedly a comedy, the film contained very few moments of intentional humour. For me, the highlight came in the first half hour, when Mrs Liscio, played by King, forgets that she has left her cat in a taxi. Not amused? Neither was I, but that was about as funny as it got.

The film tries to be a humorous semi-documentary, like a cross between *JFK*, *American Pie* and *Driving Miss Daisy*, but fails miserably to reach even the lowest depths of those films.

In terms of the quality of acting, the film also doesn't impress. King and Shaw give the impression that they've never stood in front of a camera in their lives, although the editing, which makes several continuity gaffes, doesn't help their performances. Boom microphones are frequently seen dipping in and out of shot and the shadows of the crew are visible throughout the film.

So, overall, there's nothing to recommend about this film – unless you simply want to say you've seen it. An absolute stinker – avoid at all costs.

RATING ☆ ☆ ☆ ☆ ★

Opening gives an idea of the writer's view

Summary of the topic

Topic sentences signal each stage of the review

Personal opinion

It's all about giving your opinion

When you're **writing to analyse, review and comment**, you can't really separate those writing types – they go hand in hand, as this example shows. In your SATs, they will probably crop up in the long or shorter writing tasks, in some sort of combination. You may have to analyse and comment, or review and comment – but you won't be able to get away totally from using all three types of writing at the same time. Level 5 and above writers are able to get the balance right – unlike the film-maker it seems…

Like other writing types, you need a different point in each paragraph – to show that you are analysing. That helps you to look at one thing at a time, in a <u>systematic</u> way.

To show that you are commenting, use phrases that show personal opinions – they may be formal or informal, depending on what kind of writing you are doing.

To review, look back at your subject and sum up what has happened.

I loved the director's use of humour and pathos.

It was alright I s'pose.

EXAMINER'S TOP TIPS

Organise your ideas in a clear, systematic way – plan your overall sequence of ideas, and make sure that your ideas are expressed in a logical order within your paragraphs.

Be consistent in your tone. If you want to show an extreme reaction to your subject, don't resort to silly, over-exaggerated comments, as you will lose marks for loss of control.

KEY FACTS

◄ **Give some idea of your view or intention in the opening.**

► **Summarise the topic being analysed or reviewed.**

▼ **Use <u>topic sentences</u> to signal each stage of your analysis or review.**

▲ **Include personal opinions.**

ANALYSE, REVIEW, COMMENT

- Summary
- What are you looking at?
  - Topic sentences
  - Personal opinions
- What did you think?
  - Why?
- Start
- Middle
- End
- Plan!

EXPLORE, IMAGINE, ENTERTAIN

- Grab attention!
  - Verbs
- Use descriptive techniques
  - Memorable
  - Spider diagrams
  - Lists?
- Read more!
- Lists of new words
- Start
- Middle
- End
- Plan!
- Vocabulary

WRITING

- Entertain
- Inform
- What sort?
- Varied sentences
  - Similes
  - Metaphors
  - Alliteration
  - Adjectives
  - Adverbs
- Techniques

DESCRIBE

EXPLAIN

- Purpose
  - Detail
  - So
- Therefore
- As a result
  - What's achieved?
  - Rhetorical questions
- Each point needs a reason
- Complicated ideas
  - Step by step
- Link ideas
- Varied sentence lengths
- Start
- Middle
- End
- Plan

20

ARGUE !!©!!

- Links!
- Plan!
  - Start • State your case
  - Middle • Points = Paragraphs
  - End • Reflects your argument
    - Varied openings
  - Opposite view?
- Balance • Both sides covered
  - Needn't be equal points
- Rhetorical questions

PERSUADE o Techniques
- Not all
- Use a variety
- Consider audience
- Flattery
- Emotive language
- Direct address
- Threats/blackmail
- "We"
- Rhetorical questions
- Odd one out
- Three-part repetition

TYPES

ADVISE
- Audience • Tone
  - Formal
  - Informal
- Bullet points
  - Yes?
  - No?
- Plan
  - Start • What advice?
  - Middle • Modal verbs
    - Step by step
    - Points = Paragraphs
  - End • Reasons for advice?
    - What's achieved?

INFORM
- Tone • Formal
- Plan
  - Start • What information?
  - Middle • New info = New Paragraph
  - End • Sum up
- Statistics an

Test your knowledge 1

1 There are 12 types of writing that you might be asked to do in your SATs. Name as many as you can.

Writing to...?

1 .... 7 ....

2 .... 8 ....

3 .... 9 ....

4 .... 10 ....

5 .... 11 ....

6 .... 12 ....

(12 marks)

2 In which writing type, or types, would you do the following?

a) Use flattery ....

b) Look at two sides of an issue ....

c) Use formal language ....

d) Use similes and metaphors ....

e) Give personal opinions ....

f) Use informal language ....

g) Use facts and statistics ....

(7 marks)

3 Look at these paragraphs. For each one, say what type of writing it is and identify as many features as you can that link it with that writing type, or those writing types.

Example 1
Firstly, I think that people should try to do dangerous activities for a very simple reason – the need to take on challenges. How will mankind advance if people don't try to do more difficult, dangerous things? An example of this is the recent space shuttle disaster over Texas. Although the astronauts died, we can learn from their experiences and make space flight safer in future. It is a high price to pay, I agree, but some people have to be prepared to try to dice with danger so that the human race as a whole can move forwards.

This is an example of writing to ....
I can tell because it uses

....

....

....

(4 marks)

Example 2

Surely a sensible, intelligent person like yourself should come on this climbing trip. You don't want to be the odd one out and feel awkward. It'll be perfectly safe – lots of people have done it before, so why shouldn't you? Just think how attractive you'll be to all the members of the opposite sex when you come back with your bright suntan and toned skin. I'm not asking you to come because I need someone to talk to. I'm not asking you to get full numbers on the trip. I'm asking you because I know it'll be good for you.

This is an example of writing to ....
I can tell because it uses

....
....
....

(4 marks)

Example 3

The edge of the cliff was rimmed with the azure glow of the sky. He gasped for breath and felt his heart beating against the rope with the power of a dozen brass piston engines. In his hands, the clamminess of his sweat turned cold in the chilled air against the nylon rope. He felt a mixture of unease and excitement – within a matter of moments he'd be there, a victor, a confidently commanding conqueror of this last untouched peak: the first man there. The rope jerked – he felt his foot slip and the sky moved as he lurched backwards…

This is an example of writing to ....
I can tell because it uses

....
....
....

(4 marks)

Example 4

Tryfan is one of the most well-climbed but potentially most dangerous mountains in Snowdonia. One of the easier routes to its summit begins at the Youth hostel, Ogwen Cottage at the foot of the Carneddau Mountains. From the hostel, there is a steady, but non-too difficult walk to Bwlch Tryfan, a pass between the summit of Tryfan and Bristly Ridge. From here, you scramble on all fours up a sharp ascent slightly to the south. Thereafter, there is a ridge scramble over what can be quite slippy boulders with a 3000 foot drop on both sides until you reach the summit plateau and the famous twin rocks known as 'Adam and Eve', which top the peak.

This is an example of writing to ....
I can tell because it uses

....
....
....

(4 marks)
(Total 35 marks)

I want to tell you a story...

OK, it's time to kick off this story... Are you ready?

Catchy opening

Gregory Underwood was happy. It wasn't the fulfilled man's quiet feeling that all is well with the world. It wasn't the sudden benediction granted by a moment of great triumph or unexpected good news. It was sudden, yes, unexpected – certainly – but it came from nowhere. A surge from the subconscious, a brilliance of heart and brain. He glowed.

Setting the scene

It was happening to him quite a lot these days.

His father put it down to hormones. Not that Mr Underwood – a quiet, gingery man who taught nervous housewives to drive – had any special insight into his son's mental condition. He simply observed – generally over the breakfast table – that his firstborn, in this, his seventeenth year, had grown five inches closer to the kitchen ceiling. That kind of bodily stretching was bound to stretch the mind as well. Gregory agreed. He stopped on a patch of scrubbed sward, tilting his long, lean, faintly melancholic face toward the sun. The sun was very warm. Sounds of shouting and the thudding of busy feet impinged only faintly on his consciousness. He contemplated his new state.

Range of sentence types

Details reveal features of the character

Third person viewpoint

Perhaps romance was the answer. Not that Gregory felt romantic about anyone in particular – at least anyone he stood a chance of getting to know. It was more the fact that he could, if the opportunity arose. The impulse hung in the air, vague, tremulous, unsullied by the demands of genuine experience. He wouldn't actually object to experience, as long as it was of the right kind. Nothing sordid – not too sordid, anyway. No, his soul craved something finer, something more exalted, something as enthralling as... football. His first love. As if on cue, something hard and leathery leapt out of the sun and smacked him fiercely on the forehead.

'Good header! Follow it up!'

Stunned, Gregory lurched sideways. A swarm of panting, purple-faced youths jostled past him. A football boot rasped his ankle.

'Watch yourself!' 'Underwood! Underwood!'

He turned as the swarm panted on. A spare, grim-faced man in a dark blue tracksuit beckoned from the touchline. Gregory raised questioning eyebrows.

Speech reveals the personality of the character

'When I made you a striker,' the man hissed in a stage whisper, 'I didn't mean you had to go on strike.'

OK, let's just stop the game there and see what's going on in the text. You should have learned quite a lot about the character of Gregory Underwood – and not just the fact that he's a pretty useless footballer!

The use of description helps, in this case, to create various humorous effects in creating Gregory's character. But that isn't the only thing about this that shows it is an example of **prose fiction**.

This is the start of a story. It's fiction and it's prose – but how can you tell? What are the features of the writing that give it away and help to mark it out as this particular text type? It helps if you know what sort of features there are in prose texts. These will vary, depending on the kind of texts you are given in the exam. The short answer question paper will test what you understand about texts like this and how the writer has written them.

➡ Setting the scene or character – this is done by developing the first details.

◱ A range of sentence types, ordered to achieve effects. Here, the contrast of simple and complex sentences helps the humour.

⬆ A catchy opening – in this case, it is achieved by the use of short sentences.

FEATURES OF PROSE FICTION

➡ Details that reveal features of the character or characters in the story – they often include telling adjectives, like those used here.

⬇ Speech that helps us to understand the behaviour or nature of the characters.

⬆ <u>Third person viewpoint</u> – stories are often told from the outside looking in, and this is no exception. It helps us to have an overview of the character's reactions and thoughts.

EXAMINER'S TOP TIPS

1 When looking at prose fiction, there are a number of areas that you should consider when analysing it or answering questions about it.

- What is it about?
- What viewpoint is it written from, and why?
- What kind of language and language techniques are used?
- What is the purpose or point of the writing?

2 On the SATs papers, some questions on the prose texts will ask you just to pick out examples and not explain them, some will want you just to explain quotations, and others will want you to do both. Make sure you know the difference between the types of questions when you answer. As a general rule, the 5 mark, full page questions will expect you to find quotations and use them to develop your personal opinions.

Poetry in motion

Have you ever had that Friday afternoon feeling
– that you want to get out of school, that
you've had enough, that you want to make a
move for it and run off out of your classroom?
Well, teachers feel like that too, as this poem
shows...

Last Lesson of the Afternoon

When will the bell ring, and end this weariness?
How long have they tugged the leash, and strained apart,
My pack of unruly hounds! I cannot start
Them again on a quarry of knowledge they hate to hunt,
5   I can haul them and urge them no more.
No longer now can I endure the brunt
Of the books that lie out on the desks; a full threescore
Of several insults of blotted pages, and scrawl
Of slovenly work that they have offered me.
10   I am sick, and what on earth is the good of it all?
What good to them or me, I cannot see!
So, shall I take
My last dear fuel of life to heap on my soul
And kindle my will to a flame that shall consume
15   Their dross of indifference; and take the toll
Of their insults in punishment? — I will not! —
I will not waste my soul and my strength for this.
What do I care for all that they do amiss!
What is the point of this teaching of mine, and of this
20   Learning of theirs? It all goes down the same abyss.
What does it matter to me, if they can write
A description of a dog, or if they can't?
What is the point? To us both, it is all my aunt!
And yet I'm supposed to care, with all my might.
25   I do not, and will not; they won't and they don't; and that's all!
I shall keep my strength for myself; they can keep theirs as well.
Why should we beat our heads against the wall
Of each other? I shall sit and wait for the bell.

By DH Lawrence

Metaphors, including personification

Words of the same type

Negative tone

Repetition

Writing about poetry

DH Lawrence is best known as a writer of novels. He also had a day job as a teacher, which he wasn't too keen on as you can tell from this poem! He manages to create that fed-up Friday afternoon feeling extremely well in his poem.

You may have to comment on a poem in the short answer questions paper in your SATs. It will be given as one of the texts in the reading booklet. If you are asked to write about and answer questions on **poetry**, there are some important things to remember.

EXAMINER'S TOP TIPS

Don't just spot the techniques that the writer has used - say why they have been used and what feelings they give you, if you are asked to.

Don't use lengthy quotations - keep them short and comment on individual words where you can, as this will help you to reach Levels 6 and 7.

KEY FACTS

Notice the figures of speech that DH Lawrence has used, such as:

- metaphors, including personification
- repetition
- language that creates a mood by using words of the same type – types of adjectives etc.
- the tone of the writing

Other features that are not in evidence in this poem that you might wish to comment on are:

- similes
- onomatopoeia
- alliteration
- enjambment

The rhyme structure and rhythm affect the poem in some way. This poem starts with two rhyming lines in each verse, but not in the same place. At the end, the rhymes become more regular and the poem ends with rhyming couplets. This is because it reflects the increasing boredom and repetition of the writer's day.

The viewpoint of the writer is something to consider – it affects how we react to the writer's ideas. We are seeing things from the teacher's point of view, so we take his side and feel sorry for him.

Consider how the poem is organised – is there a reason why it is or isn't in verses? Do the verses change as the content of the poem changes? Is the writer trying to achieve particular effects by the way he or she has organised the writing?

Exit stage left

Enter ROMEO

TYBALT: Well, peace be with you, sir: here comes my man.

MERCUTIO: But I'll be hanged, sir, if he wear your livery:
  Marry, **go before to field**, he'll be your follower;
  Your worship in that sense may call him **'man'**.

TYBALT: Romeo, the **hate** I bear thee can afford
  No better term than this,–thou art a **villain**.

ROMEO: Tybalt, the reason that I have to love thee
  Doth much excuse the **appertaining rage**
  To such a greeting: **villain am I none;**
  Therefore farewell; I see thou know'st me not.

TYBALT: Boy, this shall not excuse the **injuries**
  That thou hast done me; therefore turn and draw.

ROMEO: I do protest, I never **injured** thee,
  But love thee better than thou canst devise,
  Till thou shalt know the reason of my love:
  And so, good Capulet,—which name I tender
  As dearly as my own,—be satisfied.

MERCUTIO: O calm, **dishonourable, vile submission!**
  Alla stoccata carries it away.
  Draws
  Tybalt, you **rat-catcher**, will you walk?

TYBALT: What wouldst thou have with me?

MERCUTIO: Good king of cats, nothing but one of your nine
  lives; that I mean to make bold withal, and as you
  shall use me hereafter, **drybeat** the rest of the
  eight. Will you **pluck your sword** out of his pitcher
  by the ears? Make haste, lest mine be about your
  ears ere it be out.

TYBALT

I am for you.

Shakespeare and the SATs

You wouldn't want to hang around if Tybalt had got it in for you, now would you? Even if you don't know the story of Romeo and Juliet, you can still get the idea from this scene that Tybalt is not really in the best of moods and is not happy at all with Mercutio.

In your SATs you have to study two Shakespeare scenes. Each one will contain language or action about a character or theme in the same play. By looking at both scenes, you will be expected to comment on how a character changes or develops. Alternatively, you may be asked to comment on different aspects of the play or the character from each scene.

There will be different features to look at depending on which scenes and which play you study. The scenes you will have to answer questions on will be printed in your exam paper, so you won't have to memorise quotations, but you will need to understand the **language**, **characters** and **themes** in your play to get Level 5 and above.

EXAMINER'S TOP TIPS

1 Before anything else, make sure you know what happens in both your scenes and how this links to what happens both before and after in the play. In other words, make sure you know why your scenes are important.

2 Make sure you know what the key quotations are in your scenes, what they mean and all the ways in which they are important to the characters, themes and action in the play.

3 DO NOT talk about things that happened in the film version – it is the play that you have been studying!

KEY FACTS

Look at the colour-coded words and phrases in the extract to see some examples of Shakespeare's writing techniques.

1 Words that have a similar meaning or implication help to show the mood of the passage. Note all the angry violent words used by all the characters, which help to build up the tense, violent atmosphere.

2 Shakespearean language is quite similar to our own, but you sometimes need to rearrange the word order within the sentences. Here, this sentence makes more sense if you read it as 'I am not a villain'.

3 With old-fashioned vocabulary, look for connections with modern meanings to help you understand it. In this extract, 'before' means 'in front of', so Mercutio is saying to Tybalt that if he goes in front of Romeo 'to field' (as in cricket or rounders), then, and only then, will Romeo be on his side – his 'man'.

4 How the characters react towards one another helps to show how the scene relates to the rest of the play. In this extract, Romeo is pleasant towards Tybalt but, despite this, Tybalt seems to hate him. Mercutio is made angry by both of them. This helps to explain what is going to happen next – there is going to be a fight involving all three!

He seems a bit dodgy to me...

Would you want to come across this man on a dark night – or put him in a bad mood? Probably not...

Two wax candles stood lighted on the table, and two on the mantelpiece; basking in the light and heat of a superb fire lay Pilot – Adele knelt near him. Half reclined on a couch appeared Mr Rochester, his foot supported by the cushion; he was looking at Adele and the dog: the fire shone full on his face. I knew my traveller with his **broad** and **jetty eyebrows**; his **square forehead**, made squarer by the **horizontal** sweep of his black **hair**. I recognised his **decisive nose**, more remarkable for character than beauty; his **full** nostrils, denoting, I thought, choler; his **grim mouth, chin, and jaw** – yes, all three were very grim, and no mistake. His shape, now **divested of cloak**, I perceived harmonised in squareness with his physiognomy: I suppose it was a **good** figure in the athletic sense of the term – **broad** chested and **thin** flanked, though neither tall nor graceful.

Mr Rochester must have been aware of the entrance of Mrs Fairfax and myself; but it appeared he was not in the mood to notice us, for he never lifted his head as we approached.

'Here is Miss Eyre, sir,' said Mrs Fairfax, in her quiet way. He bowed, still not taking his eyes from the group of the dog and child.

'Let Miss Eyre be seated,' said he: and there was something in the **forced stiff** bow, in the **impatient** yet **formal** tone, which seemed further to express, 'What the deuce is it to me whether Miss Eyre be there or not?

Reading to analyse character

Whether you like him or not as a person, Rochester is one of the most forceful and strong characters in English literature. It is due in no small part to how Charlotte Brontë has created his character in these lines. Jane Eyre falls in love with him and, over the years, thousands of readers have done the same because he is such a wonderfully created character. She picks carefully on the most important details of his appearance and behaviour and uses them to build him up into a real person in our imagination.

EXAMINER'S TOP TIPS

Look at how description of appearance can give clues about a person's character. Read between the lines to do this.

Don't just judge a character by their behaviour. Behaviour can tell you things about character, but it is one of several things that contribute to overall character.

KEY FACTS

Look at the colour-coded words and phrases in the extract to see how Brontë creates the character of Rochester.

➡ Note the adjectives used – they help to create a sense of what the character is like.

⬇ The physical details that the writer chooses to focus on often suggest a lot about the character. Here, Charlotte Brontë focuses on Rochester's strong facial features, which imply that he is an intellectual and physical person.

↑ Background details and description help to suggest things about the character too – in this case, the background reflects Rochester's serious mood.

↩ The way that a character behaves gives an indication of his or her character. Rochester's refusal to look at Jane shows us his moodiness.

What an atmosphere!

Fog everywhere. Fog up the river, where it flows among green aits and meadows; fog down the river, where it rolls defiled among the tiers of shipping and the waterside pollutions of a great (and dirty) city. Fog on the Essex marshes, fog on the Kentish heights. Fog creeping into the cabooses of collier-brigs; fog lying out on the yards, and hovering in the rigging of great ships; fog drooping on the gunwales of barges and small boats. Fog in the eyes and throats of ancient Greenwich pensioners, wheezing by the firesides of their wards; fog in the stem and bowl of the afternoon pipe of the wrathful skipper, down in his close cabin; fog cruelly pinching the toes and fingers of his shivering little 'prentice boy on deck. Chance people on the bridges peeping over the parapets into a nether sky of fog, with fog all round them, as if they were up in a balloon, and hanging in the misty clouds.

Gas looming through the fog in diverse places in the streets, much as the sun may, from the spongey fields, be seen to loom by husbandman and ploughboy. Most of the shops lighted two hours before their time – as the gas seems to know, for it has a haggard and unwilling look.

The raw afternoon is rawest, and the dense fog is densest, and the muddy streets are muddiest near that leaden-headed old obstruction, appropriate ornament for the threshold of a leaden-headed old corporation, Temple Bar. And hard by Temple Bar, in Lincoln's Inn Hall, at the very heart of the fog, sits the Lord High Chancellor in his High Court of Chancery.

Never can there come fog too thick, never can there come mud and mire too deep, to assort with the groping and floundering condition which this High Court of Chancery, most pestilent of hoary sinners, holds this day in the sight of heaven and earth.

On such an afternoon, if ever, the Lord High Chancellor ought to be sitting here – as here he is – with a foggy glory round his head, softly fenced in with crimson cloth and curtains, addressed by a large advocate with great whiskers, a little voice, and an interminable brief, and outwardly directing his contemplation to the lantern in the roof, where he can see nothing but fog. On such an afternoon some score of members of the High Court of Chancery bar ought to be – as here they are – mistily engaged in one of the ten thousand stages of an endless cause, tripping one another up on slippery precedents, groping knee-deep in technicalities, running their goat-hair and horse-hair warded heads against walls of words and making a pretence of equity with serious faces, as players might. On such an afternoon the various solicitors in the cause, some two or three of whom have inherited it from their fathers, who made a fortune by it, ought to be – as are they not? – ranged in a line, in a long matted well (but you might look in vain for truth at the bottom of it) between the registrar's red table and the silk gowns, with bills, cross-bills, answers, rejoinders, injunctions, affidavits, issues, references to masters, masters' reports, mountains of costly nonsense, piled before them. Well may the court be dim, with wasting candles here and there; well may the fog hang heavy in it, as if it would never get out; well may the stained-glass windows lose their colour and admit no light of day into the place; well may the uninitiated from the streets, who peep in through the glass panes in the door, be deterred from entrance by its owlish aspect and by the drawl, languidly echoing to the roof from the padded dais where the Lord High Chancellor looks into the lantern that has no light in it and where the attendant wigs are all stuck in a fog-bank! This is the Court of Chancery…

Reading to analyse atmosphere, mood or tone

This foggy passage is from the opening of Charles Dickens' *Bleak House* and Dickens makes it very bleak indeed! The novel is one in which he criticises the workings of the law and the legal system in England at the time he was living. To do this, he creates a choking, threatening and overpowering mood. He didn't want just to tell people what was wrong with the law in his day – he wanted them to feel and experience it for themselves.

To do this, he builds up a powerful atmosphere that suits the mood he wants people to feel.

EXAMINER'S TOP TIPS

If you are asked to comment on atmosphere, mood or tone:

- look for similarities in vocabulary

- look for similarities between the types of words used and the subject of the passage

- look for ways in which sentence types and sentence order can help to reflect the mood

KEY FACTS

Look at the colour-coded words and phrases in the extract to see how Dickens creates atmosphere in his writing.

➡ Repetition of certain key words helps to build up a kind of hypnotic rhythm.

⬓ The length of sentences affects the reader. In this passage, the long sentences are like the fog, which is winding in and out of everywhere.

⬔ The mood reflects the story. In this passage, the description of the fog matches perfectly the feeling that someone would get if they were smothered and trapped by the 'Court of Chancery' – the place where lawsuits are sorted out and decided.

◄ Adjectives and descriptive words that have been chosen should be of a consistent type so that the mood is built up, piece by piece.

Security blanket

There are several things in life that one should never be without – and a beginner's guide to techniques used in poetry and prose is probably not one of them, except when you're about to do your SATs.

Fortunately, here's an extract from one.

Poetical and prose terms for dummies

Alliteration – the use of words starting with the same letter or sound, in close succession, e.g. 'the **d**ozy, **d**aft **d**angerous boy'.

Anaphora – the repetition of the same word or phrase at the start of a series of statements, e.g. '**without** hope, **without** care, **without** his wallet, he could not go on.'

Anticlimax – this is what happens when there is a build up of serious ideas, followed by a less serious one, often for comic effect, e.g. 'In World War Two, the Luftwaffe bombed Buckingham Palace, the houses of Parliament – and my cabbages'.

Assonance – the use, close together in writing, of words with similar vowel sounds, but different consonants, e.g. 'date' and 'fade'.

Consonance – the repetition, close together, of words with similar end consonants, e.g. 'boat' and 'night' or 'drunk' and 'milk'.

Couplet – two lines together in a poem that rhyme.

Dramatic monologue – a poem in which there is a speaker who talks directly to the reader or an imaginary audience.

Ellipsis – the use of three dots at the end of a line to suggest something obvious to the reader, e.g. 'The boy had forgotten his homework and the teacher knew…'

Euphemism – a polite way of saying something unpleasant or upsetting.

Hyperbole – deliberate over-exaggeration to highlight a point.

Imagery – words of a similar type that help to put pictures into the reader's mind.

Irony – a selection of words that are used to imply the opposite of what they literally mean, e.g. 'That's a nice jumper you've got on' snarled Kelli.

Metaphor – a kind of comparison, where one thing is said to be another, e.g. 'the steel bars of life have surrounded me'.

Narrator – the person or voice telling the story.

Onomatopoeia – words that sound like the thing they are describing, e.g. 'splash', 'bang'.

Oxymoron – contrasting ideas placed side by side to sum up confusing or seemingly opposing ideas, e.g. 'deafening silence'.

Parody – an imitation of a writer or style, but exaggerated to create humour.

Pathetic fallacy – a type of metaphor, in which inanimate objects are given human qualities, e.g. 'the cruel wind'. This is very similar to personification.

Rhetorical question – a question where the answer is suggested or implied, but not stated, e.g. 'Port Vale are brilliant, aren't they?'

Syntax – the order of words in sentences.

Poetry and prose language techniques

Knowing these terms will be very helpful in your SATs, because they will save you time. Why say that 'the writer has begun a number of words with the same letter in order to...' (15 words) when you can say 'the writer has used alliteration to...' (six words). It's much quicker and more efficient, and it will make you focus on how the writer has put his or her ideas across, which is what you are being tested on in the short answer reading paper.

slow, smooth, steps sideways
Slap! Bang! Thud!
The black cloak of night engulfed him.

KEY FACTS

1 **Writers use these techniques to create effects in their writing. You need to understand the differences between them to be able to write about them.**

2 **Looking for the use of these techniques will help you focus on how the author has written a piece.**

3 **When you are writing your own imaginative text, using some of these techniques will show creativity and will make your text more interesting to read.**

EXAMINER'S TOP TIPS

Don't just spot the techniques - say why they are being used. You will get more marks.

Make sure you can spell the terms correctly.

Make sure you understand what they mean before you comment on them.

Are you posh?

with a chill in his heart, he stared down at the body

From: mermarian@swindhold.com

Date: 1 April 2006

To: undisclosed recipients

Subject: Important request

Dear Sir or Madam – **please excuse the vagueness of the greeting**, but my uncertainty with regards to the object of my address necessitated such words.

I wish to ascertain whether you would be interested in offering administrative assistance in a joint proposal. I have recently acquired information about a lucrative business venture, which necessitates a substantial capital investment.

I have obtained the **necessary** funds, by means of contacting **trusted** business partners in my home country. These funds are **secured** in my own account in the People's Bank of Outer Mongolia.

Due to the nature of international trade laws, I cannot begin this venture outside my home country without establishing a bank account in Great Britain. I am not allowed to do this without being a citizen of the United Kingdom. As a result, I require your assistance.

If you would be so kind as to forward your bank account details, including any necessary passwords, for **validation purposes, to me, I will be able to **establish** funds in your country. This will enable my company to make a **guaranteed** profit and establish us as a respected economic concern.**

In return for your kindness, my company are prepared to offer you a 1% share of the funds that we transfer via your account and a similar share of future profits.

Please send your details via return email so we can ensure that your share of the funds reaches you as soon as possible.

Yours most humbly,

K Mermarian
Swindler Holdings
Outer Mongolia

Formal writing

Have you ever had one of these emails? Did you fall for it? Some people do, which is why they keep doing the rounds. And the reason people do is because of the way they are written – in **a formal style**.

In the SATs, you may see different styles of formal writing. You might come across it in the form of a letter, a newspaper or magazine article or an extract from an information text.

EXAMINER'S TOP TIPS

Knowing **why** the writer has chosen to write formally will help you to comment on the text you are given in the exam.

Look for polite, <u>reassuring vocabulary</u> when asked to comment on language features.

Look for modal verbs used to show politeness and respect - comment on their use!

KEY FACTS

Formal writing can be recognised by the use of certain techniques. Look at the colour-coded words and phrases in the email.

◄ **The tone is polite, so as not to offend the reader.**

➔ **The language used is often more complex than is needed in order to sound confident and assured.**

↧ **Logical and <u>sequential</u> ideas are used to suggest that the writer is reasonable.**

↥ **The use of flattery reassures the reader.**

◄ **The vocabulary used sounds safe, reliable, non-controversial and, again, reassuring.**

No, I'm common!

'Are you **lookin'** at me funny or what? Who're you **callin'** common?

Hang on a minute, I can't talk to you. I've **gorra** text from me mate.

Anyhow, who were you **makin'** fun of? I've got right trendy clothes, I'll have you know. All the best fakes off the market – don't get me **buyin'** rubbish. Me mates aren't quite so **sussed** as me. They think catalogue clothes are the business. Should see them in their plastic trainers, thinking they're **mint**. They look **right naff.**

Anyway, just cuz I come from somewhere a bit rough **don't** mean that I'm **thick.** You should see some of the kids from the posh school near me. I catch the same bus as some of 'em and you should hear some of the tripe they come out with.

They're as bad as me parents – they come out with some right embarrassing stuff in front of me mates. Me dad says things like 'You're looking fab and groovy' and me mum is just as bad. Had to tell her off for saying 'Yo dude!' when I had me mates round. Soooo embarrassing… if you're calling me common, you'd better look at them too…

Hang on, I've go' another text.

Berra go, or I'll be in big trouble. Laters!'

Informal writing

Well, some people might talk like that, and it might be a fair reflection of someone's <u>accent</u>, dialect or slang in a particular place, or at a particular point in time, but it doesn't communicate easily to a wide audience.

Informal writing is something that is quite easy to create, but is not always used to best effect.

The features used in informal writing are not 'wrong' as such – we all use them, but you have to be extremely careful how you use them. If you use them in the wrong <u>context</u>, in the wrong type of writing, you will lose a lot of credit.

Just because you use a particular word or expression, you should not assume that everyone understands it, or it is commonly used. This is particularly true of slang words and local expressions.

The misuse of informal language is one of the biggest problems that many pupils have in the SATs – make sure that you aren't one of them!

EXAMINER'S TOP TIPS

Never use too much informal language in writing tasks. Only ever use it for effect in creating characters, or addressing a familiar audience.

Never use it in formal tasks. If you are totally stuck for an expression and only a slang one will do, put it into inverted commas to show that you know you are using slang and possibly quoting, e.g. The pupils were 'gobsmacked' by the decision. If you are reading informal language, ask yourself why it is acceptable - is the audience familiar to the writer, or is it being used in fiction to create a character?

KEY FACTS

Informal writing can be recognised by the use of certain techniques. Look at the colour-coded words and phrases in the extract.

- ➡ **It contains spelling 'errors', based on how people in a particular place, of a particular age or of a social class pronounce words.**

- ⬇ **It contains grammatical inaccuracies, again based on how people in a particular place, of a particular age, or of a social class construct their sentences.**

- ⬆ **It uses shortened forms of words, often dropping endings.**

- ⬅ **It uses slang expressions that might not be understood by the whole population.**

- ➡ **It might contain its own rules of spelling, punctuation and grammar, like in text messaging.**

- Varied sentences
- Slang
- Shortened words
- Irregular spellings
- 'Incorrect' grammar

!?**!!

o Features — INFORMAL LANGUAGE

o **Why is it used?**
- Polite
- Ordered

o Features

FORMAL LANGUAGE

READING

- Give personal opinions
- Use quotations
- Pick out examples
- Explain, if necessary

o What techniques does the writer use?
- Why are they used?

o Starts and ends are important to get attention

o SATs tasks

PROSE

- Know the story
- Understand the language
- How does it affect the audience?
- Two linked scenes
- Do the characters change?
- Use quotations
- Give personal opinions

Why?
How?

DRAMA AND
SATs SHAKESPEARE

LANGUAGE TECHNIQUES

CHARACTER
- What techniques are used to create the character?
- How does their appearance affect the reader?
- How do their actions affect the reader?

TEXT TYPES AND TECHNIQUES

ATMOSPHERE, MOOD AND SETTING
- What techniques are used to create these feelings?
- Why are they used?

POETRY
- What language techniques are used?
  - Why?
- How is it organised?
  - Why?
- What viewpoint is it written from?

- Assonance
- Alliteration
- Anaphora
- Anti-climax
- Consonance
- Hyperbole
- Imagery
- Irony
- Metaphor
- Couplet
- Dramatic monologue
- Ellipsis
- Narrator
- Onomatopoeia
- Oxymoron
- Parody
- Rhetorical questions
- Syntax
- Pathetic fallacy

Test your knowledge 2

1 Write whether each of the following statements applies to 'Prose', 'Poetry' or 'Drama/Shakespeare', or any combination of them.

a) It can be written in the third person ....

b) It can be written in the first person ....

c) It can contain similes, metaphors, alliteration or onomatopoeia

   ....

d) It can be written with a narrator who talks directly to the audience/reader

   ....

e) It can contain speech ....

(5 marks)

2 Match up these technical language terms with their meanings.

| alliteration | metaphor | personification | ellipsis | hyperbole |
| onomatopoeia | parody | rhetorical question | euphemism | simile |

a) A statement in which an answer is implied or suggested

   ....

b) A statement that deliberately over-exaggerates ....

c) A statement in which something unpleasant is made to sound more pleasant

   ....

d) A word or words that sound like the things being described

   ....

e) A humorous imitation of a style or type of writing ....

f) The use of three dots at the end of a statement to perhaps create suspense or tension

   ....

g) Words close together, which begin with the same letter or sound

....

h) A comparison in which one thing is directly said to be something else

....

i) A comparison in which something non-human is given human qualities

....

j) A comparison in which one thing is said to be like another, usually using the words 'as' or 'like'

....

(10 marks)

3   In the passage below, all of the techniques mentioned in Question 2 except one are used. Which is the odd one out?

Football… it was the worst word he could have said. He had been a huge, protective emotional giant in her life. Now he seemed like a tiny mouse. Why had he mentioned football? Her least favourite sport? Her father had passed away several years ago; it had been his favourite sport and it reminded her of him.

Outside, the wind whistled sadly and it reminded her, again, of times past. It had been a billion years since she had felt highly harmoniously happy with herself. Suddenly something thudded and cracked in the corridor outside. Was it him…?

(1 mark)

4   Circle the word in each list that does not create the same mood or feeling as the others. Then write another word for each group that fits more appropriately.

a) dark, damp, delightful, dour, depressing ....

b) hot, sticky, boiling, temperate, sizzling ....

c) noisy, calm, raucous, loud, thunderous ....

d) happy, ecstatic, overjoyed, delighted, miffed ....

e) sauntering, racing, sprinting, dashing, chasing ....

(5 marks)

(Total 21 marks)

My Trip to Asia
by Stephen Cartwright

first arrived in India I was overwhelmed
intense heat. My guide took me to my w
otel, a magnificent 18th century marble

Do you need a break?

Need to get away from it all? Well, if you want a good time, a visit to Memphis in the USA might just provide the tonic you need... when you turn 21!

BEALE STREET

Beale Street began life as one of Memphis's most exclusive enclaves; its elite residents were driven out by the yellow fever epidemics, to be replaced by a diverse mix of blacks, whites, Greeks, Jews, Chinese and Italians. **But it was Beale's black culture that gave the street its fame. This was where black roustabouts, deckhands and travellers passing through Memphis immediately headed for; rural blacks came for the bustling Saturday market; and, in times of strict segregation, Beale acted as the centre for black businesses, financiers and professionals.**

As the black main street of the mid-South, Beale in its Twenties' heyday was jammed with vaudeville theatres, concert halls, bars and jook-joints (mostly white-owned). Along with the frivolity came a reputation for heavy gambling, voodoo, murder and prostitution. One appalled evangelist proclaimed that 'if whiskey ran ankle deep in Memphis... you could not get drunker quicker than you can on Beale Street now.'

Although Beale still drew huge crowds in the Forties, the drift to the suburbs and, ironically, the success of the civil rights years in opening the rest of Memphis to black businesses, almost killed it off. The bulldozers of the late Sixties spared only the Orpheum Theatre and a few commercial buildings between Second and Fourth streets.

Beale Street has now been restored as an Historic District, its shops, clubs and cafés bedecked with Twenties-style facades and signs, while a Walk of Fame with brass musical notes embedded into the sidewalk honours musical greats such as BB King and Howlin' Wolf. Tourist money has led to extensive development, but with the exception of a few out-

and-out souvenir shops, most of the new businesses remain in tune with the past, and for blues fans in particular its music venues showcase top regional talents. At its western end, 1997 saw the conversion of 126 Beale St – formerly home to Lansky's, tailors to the Memphis stars – into Elvis Presley's Memphis Restaurant, which now rivals BB King's just beyond as the street's busiest nightspot. A little further along, A Schwab's Dry Goods Store, at number 163 looks much as it must have done when it opened in 1876, with an incredible array of such voodoo paraphernalia, familiar from the blues, as Mojo Hands and High John the Conqueror lucky roots in fragrant oil, as well as 99¢ neckties and Sunday School badges (closed Sun). Next door, the free Memphis Police Museum, open around the clock, holds an assortment of old photos, newspapers and crime-fighting accoutrements – great fun at night after club-hopping.

The excellent, but peripatetic Centre for Southern Folklore (daily 11am–6pm, Sat & Sun 11am–11pm; free; tel 901/525–3655), at 119 S Main St, celebrates the music, food, storytelling and crafts of the people of the mid-South. A small stage puts on high-quality live music most afternoons or evenings, with gospel groups and choirs on Sundays, and there's also an espresso café, an exhibition area and a good gift shop that sells folk art, blues cassettes and quilts. The Centre is also home to the Shrine of the Elvis Impersonators (drop a quarter into the slot to see an assortment of would-be Elvises light up and revolve in a glittery spectacle). The comments book makes entertaining reading: in amongst the teen angst, drug-fuelled poetry and satirical doodles is the eternal question, 'If Elvis was so great, why is he buried in the back garden like a hamster?'

an astonishing blockbuster action movie with incredible special effects. From the mind-blowing title sequence to the end credits, the viewer is left gasping for air as Oscar-wiiner Arnold Stallone single-handedly takes on every bad guy in the whole world in a blistering 24 hours of mayhem before getting back in time to read his son a

2 red onions, chopped
3 sun-dried tomatoes, chopped
500g lean minced beef
salt and ground black pepper

to the meat. Cover a
simmer briskly for 5
and cook, stirring oc
until the aubergine i
and it has absorbed

Well, if you can't enjoy most of Beale Street until you're 21, then the main purpose of this text is to give you information – until you can go there and experience it for yourself!

> What are the features that show this is a **non-fiction information text**?

1 The paragraphs are clearly topic orientated – each one is on a separate aspect of Beale Street. Note the topic sentences at the start of each paragraph. That makes it easier to take in the information that you are given, and to find it again, if the information is part of a larger reference text.
2 The article contains a lot of names, facts and statistics, chosen to help the reader, in this case if they were to visit Beale Street.
3 The writing contains background information, which helps to place the facts into context. The reader can understand how all the different facts are linked or related.
4 The writer has used rhetorical questions so that the reader isn't told absolutely everything – they are made to use their imagination too.
5 Factual details are chosen carefully to intrigue and interest the reader – this is particularly important here, being part of a travel guide.

EXAMINER'S TOP TIPS

If you ask yourself some key questions about this type of text, it will help you to understand the way it has been written and organised. At Level 5 and above, good answers do this. These are often the <u>question focuses</u> on the short answer reading paper:

Decide why the passage has been written, and for whom the information is intended.

Think about why the information is organised in the order it is. Is it organised chronologically or following a physical route?

Which facts have been chosen and highlighted? Why do you think this is?

KEY FACTS

Look at the colour-coded words and phrases in the extract to see how the features are used.

▷ **Topic sentences at the start of each paragraph**

↓ **Names, facts and statistics**

↑ **Background information**

◁ **Rhetorical questions**

▷ **Factual details**

Dear Editor,
   I was appalled to re___ in your column abou
the terrible rise in this country of incidents o
antisocial behaviour at village fetes. I mysel

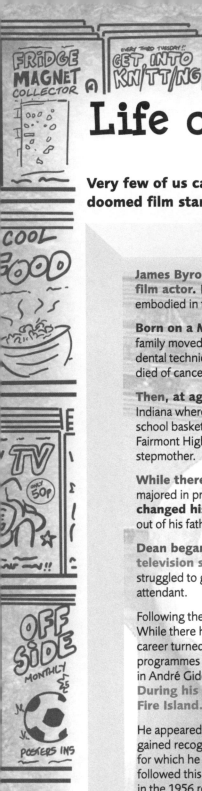

FRIDGE MAGNET COLLECTOR

COOL FOOD

TV ONLY 50p

OFF SIDE MONTHLY £5

POSTERS INS

ATCH THAT FILM

CRAZY COMIC

My Trip to Asia
by Stephen Cartwright

first arrived in India I was overwhelmed
intense heat. My guide took me to my w
otel, a magnificent 18th century marble

Life of a legend

Very few of us can look back on our lives and say we did as much as this tragically doomed film star did in a mere 24 years.

James Byron Dean (February 8, 1931–September 30, 1955) was an American film actor. Epitomising youthful angst and charisma, Dean's screen persona is probably best embodied in the title of his most representative work, *Rebel Without a Cause*.

Born on a Marion, Indiana family farm to Winton and Mildred Wilson Dean, the family moved to Santa Monica, California six years later after Winton left farming to become a dental technician. While there, Dean was enrolled in Brentwood Public School until his mother died of cancer in 1940.

Then, at age nine, Dean's father sent him back to live with relatives on a farm near Fairmount, Indiana where he was raised with a Quaker upbringing. In high school, Dean played on the school basketball team and participated in forensics debate and drama. After graduating from Fairmont High School in 1949, Dean moved back to California to live with his father and stepmother.

While there, he enrolled in Santa Monica City College, pledged Sigma Nu fraternity and majored in pre-law. **After struggling with law, against his father's wishes Dean changed his major to drama.** The resulting parental fight left Dean once again being turned out of his father's house.

Dean began his career with a soft drink commercial followed by a bit part in the television series, *Hill Number One*. He quit college to focus on his budding career, but he struggled to get jobs in Hollywood and only succeeded in paying bills by working as a parking lot attendant.

Following the advice of friends, Dean moved to New York to pursue a career in live stage acting. While there he was accepted to study under Lee Strasberg in the storied Actors Studio. His career turned around and Dean did several episodes of such early-1950s episodic television programmes as *Kraft Television Theatre*, *Danger*, and *General Electric Theatre*. His rave reviews in André Gide's *The Immoralist* led to his being called back to Hollywood and film stardom. **During his New York period he spent time in Sayville and the resort towns of Fire Island.**

He appeared in several uncredited bit roles in such forgettable films as *Sailor Beware*, but finally gained recognition and success in 1955 in his first starring role, that of Cal Trask in *East of Eden*, for which he received an Academy Award nomination for Best Actor in a Leading Role. He followed this up in rapid succession with two more starring roles, in *Rebel Without a Cause*, and in the 1956 release *Giant*, for which he was also nominated for an Academy Award.

Dean died in a road accident in a Porsche 550 Spyder when a car driven by Donald Turnupseed veered into Dean's lane. This occurred before the release of *Giant*. He is buried in Park Cemetery in his home town of Fairmount. He is one of only five people to be nominated for Best Actor for his first feature role, and the only person to be nominated twice after his death.

Dean epitomised the rebellion of 1950s teens, especially in his role in *Rebel Without a Cause*. Many teenagers of the time modelled themselves after him, and his death cast a pall on many members of his generation. His very brief career, lifestyle, violent death and highly publicised funeral transformed James Dean into a cult object and pop icon of apparently timeless fascination.

an astonishing blockbuster action movie with incredible
special effects. From the mind-blowing title sequence to
the end credits, the viewer is left gasping for air as
Oscar-wiiner Arnold Stallone single-handedly takes on
every bad guy in the whole world in a blistering 24 hours
of mayhem before getting back in time to read his son a

46

2 red onions, chopped
3 sun-dried tomatoes, chopped
500g lean minced beef
salt and ground black pepper

to the meat. Cover a
simmer briskly for 5
and cook, stirring oc
until the aubergine i
and it has absorbed

Recount texts

You may find this sort of account of someone's life in an encyclopaedia or reference book. It is known as a **non-fiction recount text** because of the way it is written. You may come across others in the short answer reading paper of the SATs.

The questions set on this kind of text are often to do with how it is organised. The language of formal recount texts can often be a bit dull because they are just factual. Biographies and autobiographies, however, often make fascinating reading, like good stories.

KEY FACTS

Look at the colour-coded words and phrases in the extract to see the features of non-fiction recount texts.

▶ **They are usually arranged chronologically, because they are dealing with a sequence of events. They are organised into sequenced/chronological topic paragraphs.**

▼ **They are very factual and contain opinions that are generally accepted and not usually very personal or controversial.**

▲ **They contain the key facts about the subject being recounted, so they are not designed to entertain, but are a type of information text.**

◀ **They use <u>connectives</u> related to time at the start of paragraphs.**

EXAMINER'S TOP TIPS

In the SATs, these types of text might crop up as part of the reading booklet for the short answer questions paper. There is often not much to say about the language of these texts, so the questions are more likely to be on their structure and organisation. To help cope with this, there are some questions you can ask yourself.

What is being recounted and why might someone want to read it?
How and why have the paragraphs been split up the way that they have?

How are the paragraphs linked?

Dear Editor,
I was appalled to re in your column abou
the terrible rise in this country of incidents o
antisocial behaviour at village fetes. I mysel

My Trip to Asia
by Stephen Cartwright

first arrived in India I was overwhelmed
intense heat. My guide took me to my w
otel, a magnificent 18th century marble

Are you following this?

Some people have a natural flair for cookery. For the rest of us, there's Delia Smith. This is one of the recipes on her website.

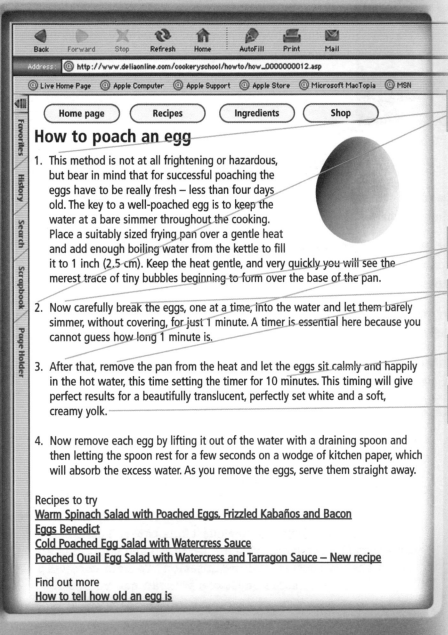

Numbered points

Time connectives

Imperative verbs

Initial instruction

Development of the idea

Address: http://www.deliaonline.com/cookeryschool/howto/how_0000000012.asp

Home page | Recipes | Ingredients | Shop

How to poach an egg

1. This method is not at all frightening or hazardous, but bear in mind that for successful poaching the eggs have to be really fresh – less than four days old. The key to a well-poached egg is to keep the water at a bare simmer throughout the cooking. Place a suitably sized frying pan over a gentle heat and add enough boiling water from the kettle to fill it to 1 inch (2.5 cm). Keep the heat gentle, and very quickly you will see the merest trace of tiny bubbles beginning to form over the base of the pan.

2. Now carefully break the eggs, one at a time, into the water and let them barely simmer, without covering, for just 1 minute. A timer is essential here because you cannot guess how long 1 minute is.

3. After that, remove the pan from the heat and let the eggs sit calmly and happily in the hot water, this time setting the timer for 10 minutes. This timing will give perfect results for a beautifully translucent, perfectly set white and a soft, creamy yolk.

4. Now remove each egg by lifting it out of the water with a draining spoon and then letting the spoon rest for a few seconds on a wodge of kitchen paper, which will absorb the excess water. As you remove the eggs, serve them straight away.

Recipes to try
Warm Spinach Salad with Poached Eggs, Frizzled Kabaños and Bacon
Eggs Benedict
Cold Poached Egg Salad with Watercress Sauce
Poached Quail Egg Salad with Watercress and Tarragon Sauce – New recipe

Find out more
How to tell how old an egg is

an astonishing blockbuster action movie with incredible special effects. From the mind-blowing title sequence to the end credits, the viewer is left gasping for air as Oscar-wiiner Arnold Stallone single-handedly takes on every bad guy in the whole world in a blistering 24 hours of mayhem before getting back in time to read his son a

2 red onions, chopped
3 sun-dried tomatoes, chopped
500g lean minced beef
salt and ground black pepper

to the meat. Cover a
simmer briskly for 5
and cook, stirring oc
until the aubergine i
and it has absorbed

Now that's a quite simple and easy-to-follow text – it's made easy by the way in which it has been structured and written.

Explanation texts

In the SATs, you are most likely to come across explanation texts in the short answer reading section. The main features of this type of text are to do with how the writing is organised, so questions may be to do with putting paragraphs in order or identifying the topics of sections of the writing.

EXAMINER'S TOP TIPS

Decide why the writing has been organised how it has. Is it chronological or is it in a series of steps connected for other reasons?

Who is the explanation aimed at? Is this reflected in the formality of the explanation? The language used in this recipe is informal because it's aimed at a beginner.

KEY FACTS

Remember these important points about explanation texts.

1 **The writing is sequential, as it has to be if there is an order to follow.**

2 **Points are made even clearer to follow by the use of numbers or bullet points, to guide the reader through the text.**

3 **Connectives used are often to do with time, because you need to follow things in a chronological sequence.**

4 **The openings of each section or explanation use an <u>imperative verb</u>.**

5 **Explanations usually contain an initial instruction, which is followed by development of the idea – perhaps a reason for the instruction, or more detailed description of the point being given.**

Dear Editor,
  I was appalled to re___ in your column abou
the terrible rise in this country of incidents o
antisocial behaviour at village fetes. I mysel

FRIDGE
MAGNET
COLLECTOR

COOL
FOOD

TV
ONLY 50p

OFF
SIDE
MONTHLY £5

POSTERS INS

ITCH THAT
FILM

RAZY
COMIC

My Trip to Asia
by Stephen Cartwright

first arrived in India I was overwhelmed
intense heat. My guide took me to my w
otel, a magnificent 18th century marble

Don't panic!

There are many serious things that people have to be prepared for. If you follow instructions on how to get ready, you will be fine.

General advice about what to do in an emergency

GO IN, STAY IN, TUNE IN

Heading

If you find yourself in the middle of an emergency, your common sense and instincts will usually tell you what to do. However, it is important to:

- (i) Make sure 999 has been called if people are injured or if there is a threat to life

- (i) Not put yourself or others in danger

- (i) Follow the advice of the emergency services

- (i) Try to remain calm and think before acting, and try to reassure others

- (i) Check for injuries – remember to help yourself before attempting to help others

Imperative verbs

If you are not involved in the incident, but are close by or believe you may be in danger, in most cases the advice is:

- (i) Go inside a safe building

- (i) Stay inside until you are advised to do otherwise

- (i) Tune in to local radio or TV for more information

Of course, there are always going to be particular occasions when you should not 'go in' to a building, for example if there is a fire.

Otherwise: **GO IN, STAY IN, TUNE IN**

The GO IN, STAY IN, TUNE IN advice is recognised and used around the world. It was developed by the independent National Steering Committee on Warning and Informing the Public as being the best general advice to give people caught up in most emergencies.

There is an agreement with radio and TV companies that if there is a major emergency they will interrupt programming to give public safety advice and information about the incident.

an astonishing blockbuster action movie with incredible special effects. From the mind-blowing title sequence to the end credits, the viewer is left gasping for air as Oscar-wiiner Arnold Stallone single-handedly takes on every bad guy in the whole world in a blistering 24 hours of mayhem before getting back in time to read his son a

2 red onions, chopped
3 sun-dried tomatoes, chopped
500g lean minced beef
salt and ground black pepper

to the meat. Cover a
simmer briskly for 5
and cook, stirring oc
until the aubergine i
and it has absorbed

SMALL, FURRY
PETS

SNOWBOARD
& TROPICAL FISH
MONTHLY

MOUSE
MAT
MONTHLY

Instruction texts

After reading that, you should be reassured that someone, somewhere has already prepared for anything that might or might not happen.

What helps with the reassurance in this extract is that the information given is in the form of **instructions**, with little explanation. That's because you probably wouldn't have much time to think, just to react, in an emergency. The instructions reflect that.

Explanations and instructions have some similar features. You are most likely to come across this kind of text in the reading test part of the SATs – the short answer questions.

SOUN
IRRITATI

KEY FACTS

1 **The instructions are usually short and don't require extra explanation.**

2 **The instructions usually start with an imperative verb.**

3 **The points are listed, often with numbers, if the instructions have to be followed in a certain order, or with bullet points, if there is no specific order.**

4 **The writer may make use of headings in order to draw the reader's eye to particular aspects of the instructions.**

5 **The tone of the instructions will depend on the audience being addressed – in the example here, the language is easily accessible because it has to be understood by the entire population of the UK, regardless of their level of education or intelligence.**

TRAI
BO
AN
PLA

COMPUTER
GAME
EXPERT

EXAMINER'S TOP TIPS

To answer questions about this type of text, there are some questions you can ask yourself.

Who are the instructions being aimed at? That will help you to understand how and why they have been written as they are. Why have they been organised in the way that they have? Are they chronological, done in order of importance or organised for some other reason?

RICE
ASHE

% OFF!
IRSDAY 12
BLE OF
ETI

Dear Editor,
    I was appalled to re n your column abou
the terrible rise in this country of incidents o
antisocial behaviour at village fetes. I mysel

LAIEJI
NEWS

FRIDGE MAGNET COLLECTOR

EVERY THIRD TUESDAY!! GET INTO KNITTING

COOL FOOD

TV only 50p

OFF SIDE MONTHLY £5

POSTERS INS

ATCH THAT FILM

RAZY COMIC

AMAZING RESCUE!! report by Sue Arms

My Trip to Asia
by Stephen Cartwright

first arrived in India I was overwhelmed intense heat. My guide took me to my w otel, a magnificent 18th century marble

Try and make me...

Controversial subjects always arouse people's strongest emotions and there is always someone wanting to persuade the rest of us that *their* view is *the* correct one to take. Hunting is one such topic that divides people into two camps.

Should fox-hunting be banned?

The Government has announced yet another attempt at fulfilling its 1997 election pledge to ban fox-hunting just as an election looms.

Our two columnists RUPERT SMYTHE and RACHEL BRADMAN couldn't wait to put across their differing opinions on the controversial issue...

HE SAYS

Our boys are dying in Iraq, poverty-hit pensioners await a particularly cruel winter, yobs rule the streets and a terror attack is supposedly imminent.

But, coincidentally, just as an election looms, Blair turns his thoughts once more, as he always does when he needs to divert attention from the real issues, to a ban on fox-hunting.

He didn't manage it last time and I predict he won't manage it this time but **it's a great headline grabber and will win back some of the woolly liberals so crabby with him about the war.**

I'd be tempted to turn the hounds on the woolly liberals themselves.

Do they not realise the traditional value of the noble sport? Do they not realise there are bigger issues at stake here?

The livelihoods of many people across the country, not just of the upper echelons of society so hated and envied by the lower classes but equally of everyday salt-of-the-earth types, depend on this tradition.

Are we to force them out of work to save the skins of a few vermin who are nothing but pests threatening to overrun the countryside, spreading disease and slaughtering sheep and chickens?

The farmers and landowners ask for nothing more than to be able to continue in their role as guardians of the countryside, unhindered by the politically correct mumbo-jumbo that seems to overwhelm our streets these days.

I suggest all the cappuccino-drinkers who are calling for a ban start getting their priorities straight and stop hating everything which was, and still is, great about our nation.

RUPERT SMYTHE

SHE SAYS

If there is a more barbaric practice on this earth, I've yet to come across it **(though no doubt Mr Smythe is also a keen bear-baiter).**

And before the pro-hunting lobby accuse me of being ignorant of country life, let me assure them I have lived in a rural retreat for a considerable length of time and have a very good understanding of what goes on.

But I still find fox-hunting to be the most **repugnant** of blood 'sports', played by people who should know better.

The same accusation could be levelled at the Government, which, given the strength of feeling against this **brutal business**, hasn't done the decent thing and slapped an outright ban on its **blood-thirsty** purveyors.

But now I hear the ban will not be imposed until 2006, so why the wait? Presumably in the hope that most of the dinosaurs involved in this most outdated of past-times have themselves passed away.

What enjoyment these people can possibly derive in seeing a fox ripped limb from limb is completely beyond me.

Which gives me an idea – why not turn the tables and set a pack of wolves on these over-privileged people and see how much fun they have?

I'm sure Rupert and his merry band of sherry-quaffing aristocrats would have a whale of a time finding out how the other half live.

Let them find out how it feels to be chased for miles by murderous hounds until you are so exhausted you can no longer move. **Then report back to me and tell me you still think it's a bit of fun.**

RACHEL BRADMAN

an astonishing blockbuster action movie with incredible special effects. From the mind-blowing title sequence to the end credits, the viewer is left gasping for air as Oscar-wiiner Arnold Stallone single-handedly takes on every bad guy in the whole world in a blistering 24 hours of mayhem before getting back in time to read his son a

2 red onions, chopped
3 sun-dried tomatoes, chopped
500g lean minced beef
salt and ground black pepper

to the meat. Cover a
simmer briskly for 5
and cook, stirring oc
until the aubergine i
and it has absorbed

Writing to persuade

These are two very strongly held views – each is trying very hard to persuade you, the reader, that they are right. Even though their views are very different, they use some very similar techniques in the way that they try to persuade the reader. They are both examples of **persuasive non-fiction**.

When you are analysing persuasive non-fiction, you will come across certain features quite frequently. You may be given such a passage as part of the reading booklet in your SATs. These features will also be useful to know for the longer and shorter writing tasks.

KEY FACTS

Look at the colour-coded text in the article to see how the main features of persuasive non-fiction are used.

◄ Rhetorical questions are used to imply the writer's point of view.

► The writers use emotive language to shock the reader into agreeing with their view.

↑ The writers show an awareness of the opposition's views, in order to try to make their views more convincing.

◄ Both writers use a memorable statement to conclude and sum up their main argument, in the hope that it lingers in the memory.

► They poke fun at the opposing view to their own.

EXAMINER'S TOP TIPS

Try to identify **how** the writer is trying to persuade the reader – that is what you will be tested on, not so much what the arguments are about.

Use quotations or specific examples to prove that you have identified these techniques and that they are actually used in the passage you're studying!

Dear Editor,
   I was appalled to re... in your column abou
the terrible rise in this country of incidents o
antisocial behaviour at village fetes. I mysel

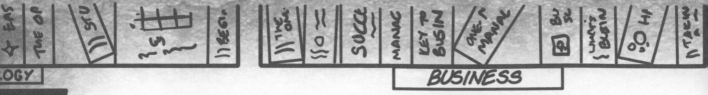
Say what you really think...

We all have opinions, and some people are actually paid to give them. The following review is from *The Washington Post*.

Robbie Fulks -
The Very Best Of Robbie Fulks

Review from The Washington Post by Curt Fields March 24th, 2000

Checking out Robbie Fulks's record collection would probably be an entertaining way to spend an evening if the influences that surface on his latest release are any indication. Fulks blends Old School country, rockabilly and bluegrass sounds with a punky pop lyrical sensibility to create songs that seldom are what they seem at first glance. It's no wonder he and Nashville couldn't get along.

Despite the title (and the hilarious but sadly untrue sources listed in the liner notes), 'The Very Best Of' is a collection of new and unreleased material that displays Fulks's idiosyncratic style at its best.

'Sleepin' on the Job of Love' sounds like **a surefire C&W radio hit – in 1972**. And yes, that's a compliment. 'Hamilton County Breakdown' **is pure bluegrass**, from his days with Special Consensus. 'May the Best Man Win' is a classic honky-tonk tune, while 'Jean Arthur' has **the same bar room sound** and anything-but-classic subject matter, namely a tribute to the actress. 'I Just Want to Meet the Man' sounds like a sentimental ballad, until you pay attention to the lyrics ('I just want to know the stranger who/Has put his poison inside of you'), at which point it takes an ominous turn.

A couple of tunes miss. The novelty of 'Roots Rock Weirdoes' grows old fast, as most jokes do. And the intentionally tasteless 'White Man's Bourbon' also wears thin fairly quickly after the title's wordplay.

But any stumbles are easily overshadowed by such gems as 'Parallel Bars' and 'That Bangle Girl'. 'Bars' is a duet with Kelly Willis about a couple that fights, goes drinking – separately – and then repeats as needed. With lines like 'She's too groovy/I love the way she sings/And I sat through her movie', 'That Bangle Girl' is a tribute to Susanna Hoffs, replete with an ohhhh-aaay-oh vocal riff that would make the Bangles proud.

If he keeps turning out work like this, there may someday be a song called 'That Fulks Boy'.

Analysing reviews

It is unlikely that Robbie Fulks would be too annoyed with what Curt Fields has said about his CD because his writing is a good example of a fair and honest **review**. Reviews are all about giving opinions, but if they are going to be well-written reviews – like the one here – they need to do certain things. If you have to analyse a review as part of the short answer reading paper in your SATs, there are certain features you should expect to see, whether the writer likes the subject of his review or not!

KEY FACTS

Look at the colour-coded text in the review to see how these features have been used.

→ It gives a factual summary of the main features of the subject of the review, in this case, the tracks on a CD, which is helpful information for the reader.

↓ Its opening creates an overall impression of the context of the review. In this review it shows where the CD fits in with other types of music. This is useful for the reader, who may or may not want to read on after this, depending on his or her level of interest.

↑ It states personal opinions and gives reasons for them.

← It uses technical language and terms that the reader of the article would probably understand. This shows that the writer is aiming his review at a <u>specialist audience</u>.

→ It balances strengths and weaknesses in order to be fair.

↓ The ending sums up the reviewer's overall feelings.

EXAMINER'S TOP TIPS

It's unlikely that you will be asked to write a review of a specific subject in the writing tasks. It's more likely that a review could turn up in the reading booklet. To get higher than Level 5, you need to ask yourself these questions.

What kind of audience is the reviewer writing for? This will affect how the review has been written in lots of ways.

What techniques has the reviewer used and why have they been used? In terms of the SATs exams, this is more important than what the review is about.

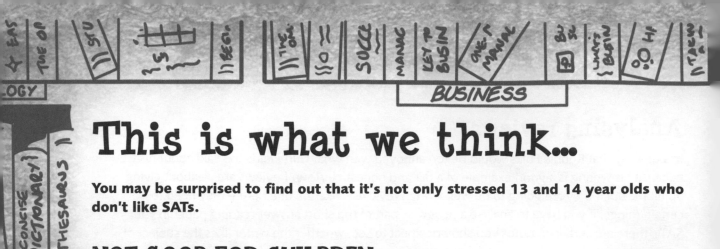

This is what we think...

You may be surprised to find out that it's not only stressed 13 and 14 year olds who don't like SATs.

NOT GOOD FOR CHILDREN
The case against national curriculum testing

Children in England are the most tested and reported on in Europe. End of Key Stage tests are taken by 1.8 million 7, 11 and 14 year olds every year. A child will take up to 105 national tests during the first 11 years.

Detailed content

Formal layout and language

Tests, targets and tables

National Curriculum tests were introduced by the Conservatives in1988. They dominate our children's education. Most teachers see them as unhelpful. They don't help children to learn. They don't help teachers to teach. They don't provide the most valuable information for parents. They aren't good for children.

Short statements

Opinions stated as facts

These tests are set at national level and have no bearing on the needs of individual schools or pupils. Marked against national standards, the results, school by school, are published annually in national school performance tables.

Parents and the public are encouraged to judge schools by these 'league tables'. Parents use them to choose schools.

What's wrong with testing?

Nothing. Teachers use their own assessments and tests regularly to assess pupils' progress and needs and to adapt their teaching. Teachers test so that they can report to parents on their children's progress. Such testing is used to help teaching. National Curriculum tests don't help teaching or children. They become the ends instead of the means.

What's wrong with National Curriculum testing?

- 'Teaching to the test' is what happens when teachers are forced not to teach to the needs of the children but to train pupils to do well in National Curriculum tests.
- So much time is spent on preparing for and taking the tests to achieve national targets that many other enjoyable and beneficial learning activities are reduced or cut out.
- Rising parental anxiety is shown by recent media reports and by commercially produced revision guides for parents moving into the top ten of non-fiction book sales.

Parents should rely on the professional judgement of teachers rather than draw conclusions from the outcomes of tests that do not properly show the achievement of their youngsters.

Advice stated as an imperative

National Curriculum tests are not helpful to teaching. They are not helpful for learning. They are not good for children! They should be abolished.

'Not Good for Children' is published by the National Union of Teachers as part of its campaign against National Curriculum testing.

Unfortunately, this is not going to get you excused from the tests. It's just one set of opinions and forms what might be called an **editorial**, or **opinion** piece. It's not balanced and reasonable because it doesn't have to be. There are lots of arguments in favour of the tests, but this article is not the place for them!

You might be asked to analyse this kind of text from the reading booklet for the short answer questions in your SATs, and you might have to write your own editorial or opinion piece for one of the writing tasks.

KEY FACTS

⬇ **Opinions stated as facts** – this can trick the reader into believing the opinion.

➡ **Formal layout and language** – this is used to make the opinions seem believable.

⬇ **Advice is stated as an imperative** – this adds weight to the opinion.

⬆ **Content is detailed** – this creates the impression that the ideas are well-researched and therefore true.

⬅ **Ideas are sequenced logically** – bullet points or lists are often used to suggest that the writer's ideas have been carefully thought out and put together.

➡ **Sentences are often short** – using single-clause matter-of-fact statements implies that there is nothing else to be said.

EXAMINER'S TOP TIPS

Knowing **how** to present your ideas is the key to getting marks when writing an opinion text. The marker wants to see you know how to construct a piece - you don't get marks for your opinions.

If you're studying a piece like this, similar advice applies - know **how** the writer has put the ideas and opinions together and comment on them. You will gain more marks if you are able to analyse how something has been written.

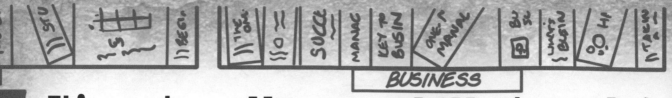

It's not really an uphill struggle!

This is one man's account of mountain climbing in the Lake District.

Although an intervening Great End had robbed us of a clear view of Scafell Pike for over 12 hours, it was still a bit of a shock next morning when we pulled up onto Esk Pike to be confronted by an entirely new and, as far as I was concerned, out-of-character face. **Our Pike had matured further, grown bulky and imposing.**

It was probably just the lighting, the way the incoming stormy clouds threw down wandering beams to pick out a cliff here, a summit shelter there; but, **as with people you at first dismiss then slowly come to admire, Scafell Pike was making an impression on me.**

After Bowfell, our route peeled off the tops and slunk south, heading away from the high mountains towards Hard Knott. It was a double blessing, for not only had the weather turned foul on lakeland's big boys, but with the growing distance came another appreciation of the Scafell massif: perspective. **And, just as the best views of Earth are from somewhere as removed as the moon, so the best views of Scafell Pike turned out to be from Harter Fell, which is where we wound up that night.**

That evening, as the Earth completed yet another of its funny turns, we were confronted by **another audible sunset**, this time with bells and whistles. It confirmed something I have long suspected: like walking in circles, most illogical ideas (sleeping on the tops – no water, exposed, hard to get to...) often turn out most sensible in the end. **The Pike may have lost its head to the clouds** but there, south of the range, we were blessed with **clear skies** and the kind of **extensive views** familiar to airline passengers.

Lying out beneath the **vast spread** of the Milky Way I felt absurdly lucky, but then this was our final night. Which was probably just as well because, as I noticed when the wind paused, we were beginning to smell.

At some point that night the winds picked up and blew down trees across Britain. We, in our three-season Tadpole tent, spent the night awake and wondering if we too were going to be blown away. We weren't, but next morning **I had bags under my eyes and the mood of a bull.** It wasn't going to be a great day.

It spat rain all morning, and the massif was lost in the cloud. Part of me was disappointed, but another small and irritatingly chirpy part said: 'And now you get to see the mountain as it looks most of the year, in cloud…' It was right, of course, and I took consolation that once again I wasn't on its flanks, but wandering through stunning Eskdale. In fact, it was so nice and rural that **by the time we came to cross into Mitterdale, I was chewing a blade of grass and contemplating a future in sheep farming.**

Not particularly realistic I'll agree, but it does go to show how walking can turn you from a **tired, angry man** to a **happily deluded optimist** in the space of a few hours. If I could, I'd put it in a bottle and sell it in a trendy boutique in Covent Garden. It's the ultimate route to tranquillity.

Ben Winston, From Trail Magazine, November 2004

As tiring and as troublesome as the journey up Scafell Pike seems, Ben Winston also conveys a tremendous enthusiasm for his subject in the way that he describes the whole experience.

In this way, **non-fiction description** has a great deal in common with fictional description – except that it's for real!

EXAMINER'S TOP TIPS

If you are given a non-fiction descriptive piece as part of a reading task, analyse it as you would analyse a piece of fiction. Think also of the purpose of the writing, as that's the main difference between the two.

If you have to write a non-fiction descriptive piece, remember to think about how you will organise it and make it clear who you are writing for.

KEY FACTS

Non-fiction description writing has many features. Look at the colour-coded text in the article to see how the writer has used them.

➡ **Figurative language**, such as metaphors and similes, is used.

⬇ **Personal opinions and insights add interest.**

⬆ **Descriptive words and phrases are chosen to create moods and feelings.**

⬅ **The writing in this case is organised in a chronological manner, as it is an account of a personal experience.**

➡ **Paragraphs are linked by connectives to do with time and place, as the writing in this case is chronological and based on a description of a particular area.**

⬇ **The writer of this piece has made it accessible for a wide audience with all these techniques, but the use of place names makes it more suitable for a specialist reader who knows the areas being described.**

READING

INFORMATION

- Paragraphs = Topics
- Choice of details
- Names, facts, statistics
- Background information
- Rhetorical questions
} o Features

- Who has written it?
- Why?
- Who for?
- Why have these facts been chosen?
} o SATs

EXPLANATION

- How is it organised?
- Why?
- Who is it aimed at?
- How can you tell?
} o SATs

- Chronological
- Sequenced
- Bullet or numbered points
- Time connectives
} o Features

INSTRUCTIONS

- Who is it aimed at?
- Why is it written as it is?
} o SATs

- Tone
- Headings
- Imperative verbs
- Short sections
- Vocabulary suits audience
} o Features

PERSUASION

- Make fun of opposition
- Memorable start and end
- Rhetorical questions
- Use opposing views to destroy them
- Emotive language
} o Features

- How is the reader persuaded?
- How successful is it?
- Why?
} o SATs

DESCRIPTION

○ SATs
- Who is it written for?
- How can you tell?

○ Features
- Vocabulary
- Descriptive words
- Mood
- Setting
- Personal opinions
- Figurative language

TEXT TYPES AND NON-FICTION

RECOUNT

○ Features
- Often chronological
- Often factual
- Paragraphs = Topics
- Often connectives related to time

○ SATs
- What is it about?
- Why?
- How are the paragraphs linked?
- Why?

REVIEWS

○ Features
- Balance
- Personal opinions
- Put subject in context
- Summary
- Technical language used

○ SATs
- What techniques
- Why?
- Who is it written for?
- How can you tell?

ICE NEW TECH MAGAZINE

NEW CD IS BEST Y

EDITORIAL/ OPINION

○ Features
- Often logical order
- Detailed
- Opinions stated as facts
- Short sentences
- Advice
- Uses imperatives

- How have the ideas been presented?
  - How well?
  - Why?

Test your knowledge 3

1   Match the text features with the text types below. Some text features apply to more than one text type.

Text features

a)   Ideas are often ordered in a logical sequence ....

b)   The writing includes reasons ....

c)   The writing may be biased ....

d)   Many sentences start with imperative verbs ....

e)   The writing often makes use of adjectives, adverbs, metaphors or similes

....

f)   The writing might include a summary ....

g)   The writing contains personal opinion ....

h)   The writing might contain facts and statistics ....

Text types:	Information	Recount
Explanation	Instructions	Persuasion
Review	Editorial/Opinion	Description

(8 marks)

2   For each paragraph, decide which non-fiction text type you think it is. Then give three reasons for your decision.

Paragraph 1

The film 'The Crow' is one of the finest modern gothic films you will see. Its dark scenes, hints of horror and evil, along with its loud and lively soundtrack, make for a perfect afternoon's viewing in a darkened room, especially if you're a teenager who likes to wear black. Older and younger viewers might not appreciate its references to goth culture and its thudding audio, but then those people probably won't be flocking to watch it. Overall, a cracking film, but mainly suitable for those in their mid to late teens. Four and a half stars!

This is an example of writing to ....
I can tell this because it uses

....

....

....

(4 marks)

Paragraph 2

Firstly, remove the packaging. Your new studio monitor speakers must be allowed to adjust to room temperature. Allow them to sit in the room that they are going to be used in for a couple of hours. Next, place the speakers on their stands. Make sure that they are correctly aligned, by using a spirit level. Attach the speakers to your amplifier with the included phono cables. Ensure that you turn on the speaker marked 'A' first, before switching on speaker 'B'.

This is an example of writing to ....
I can tell this because it uses

....

....

....

(4 marks)

Paragraph 3

The Sears Tower in Chicago is a surprising building – not easy to spot from amidst the Loop's skyscrapers, its top often gets lost in the gloomy clouds that roll in incessantly off Lake Michigan, carried by the icy draughts that give the Windy City its name. On closer inspection, it's a real neck breaker – try standing at its foot and peer hopefully at the upper floors and you're likely to find yourself giddily rocking backwards. From the nose-bleedingly high observation deck, its views are stunningly varied and you'll say to yourself, 'Yes, those are clouds below me, and yes, this building is wobbling!'

This is an example of writing to ....
I can tell this because it uses

....

....

....

(4 marks)

Paragraph 4

This newspaper stands up for what is fair and just and this latest issue is one that we could not ignore. Why should boys not be allowed to wear skirts in school? If girls are allowed to wear trousers, why is the reverse not true? Surely, those who argue that it's unnatural or wrong are the ones who are narrow-minded and in the wrong. Here at the *Weekly Mail*, we feel that equality is more important than fashion or personal opinion. Join our campaign – claim a free sticker from your local newsagent today. Be proud, be loyal, be a skirt wearer!

This is an example of writing to ....
I can tell this because it uses

....

....

....

(4 marks)

(Total 24 marks)

Mnemonics might be necessary

According to the Guiness Book of Records, there is a word with more than 207,000 letters. Fortunately, you do not have to learn how to spell this word. However, you do need to know how to spell other words and there are strategies to help you do this.

Mnemonics

A mnemonic is a memorable sentence made up from every letter of a word, in order.

Look at this example:

Not **E**very **C**hild **E**asily **S**ucks **S**weets **A**nd **R**aces **Y**achts

If you look at the first letter of each word in the phrase, it spells the word 'necessary'.

Here are some examples of mnemonics for words you might use in the reading tasks:

simile – Silly Imbeciles Might Ingest Lovely Eggs

biased – Brian Is A Small Eared Dimwit

metaphor – Meat Eaters Taste Amazing Pies, Hung Off Rods

alliteration – All Ladies Like Interesting Tales, Except Rodney's, And That Is Only Normal

Try making up some of your own for these words:

Oxymoron   Couplet   Euphemism   Rhetorical

Banquo   Macbeth   Benedick   Claudio

Spell-speak

Another method you might use to help you remember spellings is to break words down into parts and use something called 'spell-speak'. Spell-speak is where you pronounce the word in the way that it is written, not the way that it is properly pronounced. This makes you exaggerate the correct spelling, which, in turn, helps you to remember it.

Here is an example:

definite – def–in–ite

It has three parts, or syllables. If you pronounce the last syllable as 'ite', as opposed to 'it', when you say it to yourself, it will help you to remember the tricky part of the spelling.

Here are some more examples:

recommend – re–com–mend   Remember to pronounce the consonants in the middle!
independent – in–de–pen–dent   It's important to exaggerate the 'e' sounds.

Try turning these into spell-speak:

language   **repetition**   **separate**   **desperate**   **onomatopoeia**

Words within words

Spelling some words can be mastered if you can find another word inside the main word you're trying to spell. You can then build it up from that by adding extra letters, prefixes and suffixes. Take this commonly misspelled word:

Disappear – dis + appear   If you know how to spell 'appear', then just add the prefix 'dis'.

You can build up other words in blocks like this – it doesn't have to be the root word that helps you with the spelling.

achievement – achieve + ment
mathematics – ma + them + atics
permanent – per + man + ent

Try looking for the words within words in these examples:

narrator   **piece**   **perseverance**   **missile**   **prescription**

EXAMINER'S TOP TIPS

Go through your own spelling mistakes in your schoolwork. Make a list of words that you have problems with. Use mnemonics, spell-speak or words within words to try to find ways of remembering them.

Keep a log of words that you have problems with and keep updating it. In the run up to the SATs, make an effort to learn the words that you might need in the exams, such as technical terms to do with language or names of Shakespearean characters.

Spelling rules, OK!

Henry Dark was worried. He had just had his essay back from his teacher and it was covered from top to bottom with red ink. The teacher had put one comment at the bottom. It read: 'HENRY! LEARN YOUR SPELLING RULES!'

But he didn't know any spelling rules, so how could he learn them? He was about to give up, as his confidence had taken a real battering, when he spotted a piece of crumpled paper on the floor of the classroom. By a stroke of luck, it was a list of spelling rules.

It was a ray of hope. All Henry had to do was to match up the rules with his own mistakes and then he would be able to see where he'd gone wrong.

This is Henry's essay:

I walkd slowley to the front door. I was haveing an absolute nightmare. I wantd to run of and never come back. Their was a strange fealing in the air. I would have happyly racet away at that very moment and found my freinds. The leafs where rustleing behind me and the trees were shakeing.

If the path had been accessable, I would have run their and then, but it wasn't, so I couldn't. I was trappt with nowere to go. My dependible freinds had left me.

Suddenley, they're was a loud crack from behind me. The storys about this place seamed to be true. I was shure it was hornted. I thought about the places I'd visitd before — the old churchs and the lonly beachs, but non had scard me like this place...

I herd another noise. This time it was geting closer. Hot sweet was trickleing down my back. I quickley turnd and their it was...

Here's the list of spelling rules that Henry found. Read them through and try to correct Henry's essay for him.

Spelling rules

- Add 'ed' onto verbs that end with a double consonant, in order to make the past tense.

- To make an adjective into an adverb, add 'ly'. If the adjective ends in 'y', change the 'y' to 'i' before adding 'ly'.

- To add 'ing' to verbs that end in 'e', take off the 'e' and add 'ing'.

- To add 'ing' to verbs that end in vowel + consonant, double the consonant before adding 'ing'.

- Don't confuse 'of' (belonging to) and 'off' (away).

- Be careful not to confuse homophones – words that sound the same, but are spelled differently and have a different meaning.

- Nouns that end in 'ch' or 'sh' usually add 'es' to form the plural.

- Change 'y' to 'i' and add 'es' to make the plural of nouns that end in consonant + y.

- 'i' before 'e' except after 'c'.

- Watch out for silent letters.

- If you remove '-able' from a word, you are left with a complete word.

- If you remove '-ible' from a word, you are not left with a complete word.

- Learn the difference between words using 'ee', 'ea' and 'ie' to make an 'e' sound.

EXAMINER'S TOP TIPS

Find a couple of pieces of recent written work that you've done. Go through them as you did with the passage above and see which rules you break.

Make a list of priorities - if there are a lot of rules that you break, concentrate first on those that you break most frequently.

If you're not sure which rule you're breaking, get a dictionary and learn the word - sometimes, there's no easy way!

Spot the full stop

If you think Henry Dark is bad at spelling, then you should see Morgan Calamity's punctuation. The poor boy wouldn't know a full stop if it came up and thumped him on the forehead! He keeps getting his apostrophes in a twist and you don't want to know about the state of his semi-colons.

This is his latest piece of work. The teacher asked him to punctuate a simple sentence.

Poor old Morgan got into a fair old flustered state. Firstly, he wrote it this way:

But then he had second thoughts and re-did it this way:

He couldn't decide which one was correct. To be honest, they are both correct – it just depends what he wanted to say. What it showed him was the importance of punctuation. As this example shows, punctuation affects – and can totally change – the meaning of a sentence. That's why it has more marks allocated to it than for spelling in the SATs exam!

Have a look at this example of Morgan's music homework.

bobby bare junior is the son of the famous singer bobby bare he was brought up in nashville tennessee he had duetted with his dad on the song daddy what if written by family friend and mentor shel silverstein on the senior bares album lullabies legends and lies
   when he got older with his band bare jr he put out two albums full of angstfilled hookladen, poison pen rock this didnt go down very well so he returned to the basics with his side project band called the young criminals starvation league they signed to chicagos bloodshot records and enjoyed a lot of critical success

Thankfully, Morgan's music teacher was able to help. She handed him this piece of paper.

A Guide to Punctuation

1 Use capitals for names, titles and starts of sentences.
2 Full-stops are needed at the ends of sentences. A sentence is a group of words that make complete sense on their own.
3 Commas separate items in lists and also clauses, where extra information or asides are added to sentences.
4 Semi-colons are used to connect complete sentences; extra information is given after them.
5 Inverted commas are used for speech and quotations.
6 Hyphens are used to connect compound words.
7 Apostrophes are used for missed out letters.
8 Apostrophes are also used to show possession.
9 Start a new paragraph when you start a new topic.

Based on this excellent advice, Morgan corrected his passage and this is what he produced.

> Bobby Bare Junior is the son of the famous singer Bobby Bare. He was brought up in Nashville, Tennessee. He had duetted with his dad on the song 'Daddy, What If?' written by family friend and mentor, Shel Silverstein on the senior Bare's album, 'Lullabies, Legends and Lies'.
>
> When he got older, with his band Bare Jr, he put out two albums full of angst-filled hook-laden, poison pen rock; this didn't go down very well, so he returned to the basics with his side-project band called The Young Criminals Starvation League. They signed to Chicago's Bloodshot Records and enjoyed a lot of critical success.

If you compare Morgan's original draft with his improved version, you should find one example of each rule being applied. It's a great deal better, makes much clearer sense and would help him get higher marks in a SATs exam.

EXAMINER'S TOP TIPS

Look at a couple of recent pieces of extended writing that you've done. Can you find an example of each of the above rules that you have (a) got right and (b) got wrong?

Make a list of your most common mistakes and use the rules and examples here to help correct them.

Stay on topic!

Zoe Elliot was a chatterbox. She talked a lot, and very quickly, hardly pausing for breath. When she wrote, it was like she was talking. She wrote pages and pages of full lines, never using paragraphs to start a new topic.

Here's a typical example of her work.

'A dog is man's best friend.' Many people agree with that, but many don't. In this essay, I am going to explain why I disagree. In the first place, people enjoy the company of cats. Many cats are friendly. Who can resist a purring cat? If they're not feeling affectionate, cats are generally quite lively. They love to chase balls and feathers, or just about anything dangling from a string. They especially enjoy playing when their owners are joining in. Secondly, contrary to popular opinion, cats can be trained. Using rewards and punishments, just like with a dog, a cat can be trained to avoid unwanted behaviour or perform tricks. Cats will even fetch things! My next point is that cats are civilised occupants of the house. Unlike dogs, cats do not bark or make other loud, annoying noises. Most cats don't even purr very often. They generally lead a quiet existence. Cats also don't often have toilet 'accidents'. Mother cats train their kittens to use the litter box, and most cats will use it from that time on. Even stray cats usually understand the idea when shown the box, and will use it regularly. Lastly, one of the most attractive features of cats as house-pets is their ease of care. Cats do not have to be walked. Cats are low maintenance, civilised companions. People who have small living quarters or less time for pet care should appreciate these characteristics of cats. However, many people who have plenty of space and time still opt to have a cat because they love the cat personality. In many ways, cats are the ideal house-pet.

Zoe's teacher thinks her work could be improved. He gave her this advice:

Start a new paragraph when you start a new topic or idea.

Zoe went back to her work and put in paragraphs based on this advice.

'A dog is man's best friend.' Many people agree with that, but many don't. In this essay, I am going to explain why I disagree.

In the first place, people enjoy the company of cats. Many cats are friendly. Who can resist a purring cat? If they're not feeling affectionate, cats are generally quite lively. They love to chase balls and feathers, or just about anything dangling from a string. They especially enjoy playing when their owners are joining in.

Secondly, contrary to popular opinion, cats can be trained. Using rewards and punishments, just like with a dog, a cat can be trained to avoid unwanted behaviour or perform tricks. Cats will even fetch things!

My next point is that cats are civilised occupants of the house. Unlike dogs, cats do not bark or make other loud, annoying noises. Most cats don't even purr very often. They generally lead a quiet existence. Cats also don't often have toilet 'accidents'. Mother cats train their kittens to use the litter box, and most cats will use it from that time on. Even stray cats usually understand the idea when shown the box, and will use it regularly.

Lastly, one of the most attractive features of cats as house-pets is their ease of care. Cats do not have to be walked. Cats are low maintenance, civilised companions. People who have small living quarters or less time for pet care should appreciate these characteristics of cats. However, many people who have plenty of space and time still opt to have a cat because they love the cat personality. In many ways, cats are the ideal house-pet.

If you look at the beginning of each paragraph, you can see that phrases have been used that help to show a new point is being introduced, e.g. 'In the first place', 'Secondly', 'My next point' and 'Lastly'. They almost number the paragraphs.

The paragraph openings used are not very imaginative. If you are aiming for a higher level in the writing tasks, you will need to vary your paragraph openings.

EXAMINER'S TOP TIPS

Plan your writing, so that you remember to paragraph. Each paragraph in your writing should cover one point in your plan.

Use a variety of paragraph openings, especially if you want to score the highest levels in your SATs.

KEY FACTS

1 **Start a new paragraph when you start a new topic or idea.**

2 **Using simple, straightforward paragraph openings shows you have grasped the basics of paragraphs. To show greater skill as a writer, use a wider variety of paragraph openings.**

Examples are:

⬇ Primarily	➡ In addition to this	⬇ Furthermore	⬆ In opposition to this
⬇ To conclude, I would suggest	➡ Subsequently	⬇ Often	⬆ Usually

Super structure

Well structured work gets higher marks. This top secret document shows how and why. It is the section on structure from the Key Stage Three mark scheme.

This section focuses on how overall meaning and effect is put across through the way that the writing is organised and planned.

Band B1

Ideas are mainly linked because they happen to be on the same topic.
Points might be put in a list, but not necessarily in any sort of order of importance.
Paragraphs might be used to show some of the obvious different topics in the writing.

0 marks

Band B2

Paragraphs usually start with the main topic in the first sentence.
The paragraphs will contain examples.
The text has some brief opening and closing comments, but they will be fairly brief and undeveloped.

1 or 2 marks

Band B3

Paragraphs are written in a logical order.
The introduction and conclusion are clear.
Paragraphs of different lengths are used, e.g. short paragraphs might take the form of a persuasive question.

3 or 4 marks

Band B4

Detailed content is well handled within and between paragraphs.
Some phrases like 'On the other hand' or 'In addition to this' etc. are used to link the paragraphs.
The introduction and conclusion to the text are developed and help to make it more persuasive.   5 or 6 marks

TOP SECRET

Band B5

Paragraphs are varied in length to suit the different ideas being discussed.
The paragraphs are linked with a variety of words and phrases.
Paragraphs are ordered in such a way that the writer might have used them to highlight contrasts, or to be ironic.   7 marks

Band B6

CONFIDENTIAL

The whole piece of writing is organised, shaped and controlled to achieve a range of effects, or to get the reader thinking in a certain way.
Within paragraphs, the writer has used a wide range of links that are precisely and carefully chosen.   8 marks

If you've done your detective work, you should have noticed that each band has two or three strands and these strands cover the following:

- paragraphs
- links between paragraphs
- the way words and ideas are organised within paragraphs
- the overall shape and structure of the writing

KEY FACTS

◁ If you follow these points, you will be able to structure your work well and that will help you get as many marks as possible.

⊡ Decide what is going to happen at the beginning, middle and end of your writing.

⬇ Plan the order in which you are going to put your ideas.

⬆ Plan the order of ideas in each paragraph.

◁ Think about how you are going to start each paragraph. Use phrases that start a new topic, yet link to the paragraph before.

⊡ Try to vary the lengths of paragraphs. Use some short ones for shock effect.

EXAMINER'S TOP TIPS

Planning is the key to success and higher marks.

Decide what you are going to write about and how it will be structured before you start.

Variety is the spice of life

Life gets very boring if you always do things the same way. Variety, they say, is the spice of life.

Variety in writing was Dan Holway's biggest problem. Every sentence of his started with a main clause. If you were lucky, he would grace you with a subordinate clause too, but that was about it.

In short, his writing was boring – dull, dull, dull. Here is an example of Dan's writing:

I went to the corner shop. I bought some food. The food was tasty. Afterwards, I went to a football match. Port Vale were playing Sheffield Wednesday. The match was a good one. It ended up a three–three draw. Then I went home. I had my tea. I watched the television and then I went to bed.

It's quite obvious to me that Dan's sentences need a serious makeover. Let's start with the opening line.

I went to the corner shop.

It's a noun and a verb and it makes sense, but that's about it. Why don't we put in a couple of adjectives to start with?

I went to the rundown, dirty corner shop.

Much better, but it's still a straightforward sentence. Let's combine it with the second sentence by turning it into a subordinate clause.

I went to the rundown, dirty corner shop to buy some food.

Why don't we lash on some more adjectives and, dare I say it, an adverb?

I went wearily to the rundown, dirty corner shop to buy some greasy, satisfying food.

Now that I look at it, it might look better if we turn it around.

In order to buy some greasy, satisfying food, I went wearily to the rundown, dirty corner shop.

Look at the last two examples again. Which one would you pick if you wanted to create a feeling of tension? It would probably be the last one because it delays the reader finding out where the person in the sentence is going. If you can write a sentence like that, you're well on the way to being able to create variety in your sentences.

In the mark scheme for the SATs, you'll gain up to eight marks on each of the writing tasks by varying your sentences. On the longer writing task, the marks are just for that, but on the shorter writing task the marks are part of the section that includes punctuation and paragraph organisation.

Following the examples here will help you bring more variety to your own sentences. You can practise by having a go at improving the rest of Dan Holway's passage. Try not to make two sentences sound the same. Mix them around and see what effects you can achieve. The more you do this, the more confident you will become in writing such sentences from scratch.

KEY FACTS

- Make your sentences as varied as possible. Some can be short with a single clause, while others should be more complex with one or more subordinate clauses.

--- --- --- --- --- --- --- --- --- ---

- Use adjectives to make your nouns more interesting.

--- --- --- --- --- --- --- --- --- ---

- Use adverbs to make your verbs more interesting.

--- --- --- --- --- --- --- --- --- ---

- Use the structure of your sentences as well as the words in them to create effects on the reader.

--- --- --- --- --- --- --- --- --- ---

EXAMINER'S TOP TIPS

Don't be scared to cross things out and make changes on the exam paper. If you can't think of a good sentence at first, change it later. You won't lose or gain any marks for tidiness, as long as your words can be read.

When you change things, do proofread to make sure they make sense.

It depends where you're standing

These three paragraphs are all about the same person, but there's a difference...

I often go to the movies. Winonie Bryder and Reese Wetherspoons are two actresses who I admire for their acting skills and for their ability to project star quality. I also admire the fact that they're stunningly attractive and, given half a chance would surely want to marry me – or at least go out with me. I can't help it if I'm stunningly handsome. I can't help it if women throw themselves at my feet, can I?

Do you think that's clever? Do you think that is an appropriate attitude to take? You must be joking. You should never talk like that – what will people think? You seem to have a very high opinion of yourself.

Did you work out what the difference was between the paragraphs? They are written from different viewpoints.

- The first paragraph is written in the **first person**.
- The second paragraph is written in the **second person**.
- The third paragraph is written in the **third person**.

What difference does that make? Look at what we learn about the character, Godfrey, in each of these paragraphs.

People who show off and brag in public are often quite insecure. My daughter was always saying that about our neighbour Godfrey. He used to brag about how much of a lady-killer he was. She thought he was just covering up for the fact that he lived a sad, lonely life and he was trying to make people believe he really was a 'someone'.

In the first person version, he comes across as arrogant and is obviously very conceited. His own words give us this feeling. That's the main advantage of the first person viewpoint – the reader is close to the emotions, feelings and actions of the person telling the story or giving the account. This viewpoint is good for getting inside a character's head. You can have a first person narrator who comments on the other characters in the story.

The second person viewpoint is not a very common one. It might be used if you were writing a <u>monologue</u> and were speaking directly to the audience. Like writing in the first person, it reveals as much about the speaker as the topic being discussed.

The third person viewpoint is good for giving an overview and for commenting on things from a detached viewpoint. In the third paragraph above, the third person narrator is able to give us a range of opinions and interpretations of attitudes and events.

> I would like to ask which viewpoint to choose! (First person)

> You want to ask about the viewpoint? (Second person)

> At this point the readers were getting curious about which viewpoint should be used. (Third person)

The viewpoint you choose largely depends on the type of task you are set. There are no hard and fast rules for what is right or wrong.

A story, for example, could equally be told from a first or third person viewpoint. A persuasive speech might be written in the first person to make it more passionate and determined, but it could equally be written in the third person to make it seem unbiased and reasonable.

EXAMINER'S TOP TIPS

Choose a viewpoint that seems realistic and appropriate for the task set. The marker isn't looking for one specific viewpoint or another.

Once you have chosen your viewpoint, stick to it. If you change viewpoints in your writing, under exam conditions, your writing will almost certainly sound confused and you will lose credit.

KEY FACTS

1 When you write in the first person, you are talking about yourself, e.g. I did this, I saw that.

2 In the second person, you talk to someone, e.g. you were working late, what were you thinking?

3 In third person narrative, you talk about other people, e.g. the dancers were exhausted, he enjoyed cycling.

Seeing red

A new reporter has just presented his first piece to the senior editor. Here's why he didn't last till the end of the week...

Building plan causes outcry

elevation

plan view

PLAN FOR NEW LIBRARY FACILITY

Plans for a contravershal extension to the library led two a public disturbance, when they where unveiled at Wednesday's council meeting.

A group of individuals, claiming the building will damage the enviroment, suprised the ussually quiet weekly meeting by storming the building in a desparate attempt to embarass the mayor and sway public oppinion.

The group claims the building plans our benifishal too no-one and labelled the Green Party council members as hippocrytes.

In a statement the mayor said: "The plans we're approved by unanimus decision, and there ridiculous display has acheived nothing."

Common spelling errors

These are the correct spellings! Use the strategies discussed previously to try to learn the ones that you think you might need.

absence	controversial	intellectual	probably	surprise
accidentally	desperate	loneliness	receive	tragedy
achievement	embarrass	opinion	recommend	tries
appearance	environment	optimistic	repetition	unanimous
argument	exaggerate	parallel	ridiculous	unnecessary
beneficial	fascinate	possession	separate	usually
changeable	government	possibility	similar	weird
conscience	hypocrite	prejudice	sincerely	whether

Homophones

Another common mistake is the confusion created by homophones – words that sound the same, but are spelled differently and have different meanings. With these, you only need to find a way of remembering one of the spellings and meanings. Then you should be able to work out which word you need.

Hear/Here
Hear – has the word 'ear' inside it, and is to do with listening
Here – in this place

There/Their
Their – is linked to the word 'they'. It is similar to other possessive pronouns like 'our' and 'your' in that it ends in 'r'

There – in that place. It contains the word 'here' and is to do with a place.

Your/You're
Your – belonging to you. It is similar to other possessive pronouns like 'our' and 'their' in that it ends in 'r'

You're – has an apostrophe in it, so it must mean 'you are'. If you're still not sure, try putting 'you are' in place of your/you're. If it makes sense, you need 'you're'; if it doesn't, you need 'your'.

Stationery/Stationary
Stationery – paper, pens, pencils etc. It has an 'e' for envelope in it.
Stationary – standing still

To/Too/Two
To – used in directions and before the infinitive form of the verb, e.g. I am going to the doctor. To be or not to be?
Too – used with amounts, e.g. too much, too soon
Two – the number 2

Are/Our
Are – We are interested in science.
Our – It is our science book.

Which/Witch
Which – Which one is it?
Witch – The witch in the black hat.

Other common confusions

A lot – meaning many – is two separate words

Could have – NOT 'could of'. If you were writing this as speech, it would be 'could've'.

It's – it is. The apostrophe stands for the missing 'i'.
Its – belonging to it – no apostrophe!

Lose – to mislay, be defeated
Loose – slack, sloppy

Were – past tense of 'are'
Where – asks about a place, like 'there' and 'here'
We're – we are – remember the apostrophe
Wear – what you do with clothes

EXAMINER'S TOP TIPS

An exam marker's impression of how accurate you are as a writer will be based on how successful you are at avoiding the errors described here. Create the right impression by learning the correct spellings.

Computer spellcheckers can't spot homophones used incorrectly, so get into the habit of proofreading your own work.

Pace yourself

Don't revise for long periods at a time. Revision is best applied like exercise – it needs to be done regularly, in manageable doses of about 15 to 20 minutes. In between revision sessions, give yourself a mental and actual break for five to ten minutes.

Location matters

Make sure you study in a suitable place – that will vary, depending on what helps you to concentrate. Some people need silence, while others find that background music helps to shut out disturbance and keeps them focused.

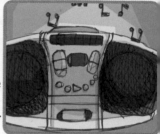

Preparation

How to revise

Plan

Make a revision plan. Draw up a calendar and mark on the nights and/or times when it's going to be difficult to do any meaningful revision.

Focus

Prioritise those things that you need to revise more than others and mark them on your plan first. Look at targets you have been given by your teachers and use them to help plan and focus your revision.

Working with friends

- If you are easily distracted and can't really trust yourself to work, this will not work for you.
- If you are disciplined enough, why not test each other? Make the revision competitive – who can get the most correct?
- Make revision materials together. Theoretically, you should be able to produce at least twice as many.

Use the tests in this book!

They are designed to make sure you know what is required in terms of your reading and writing skills for the exams. If you can do the tests in here, you're on the right lines. There's nothing wrong, either, in re-testing yourself on the same questions. If you can see how and why you did better on a second or third occasion, that's useful revision and progress.

Post-it notes

Write your revision tips and information on post-its and stick them in places where you are likely to see them a lot.

Organise your post-its – put spelling ones by the mirror, punctuation ones around your bed and so on, so that you come to associate certain places with certain tips or information. If you get stuck, visualise the place to help you remember.

Methods of revising

Use a variety of revision methods to keep your revision fresh.

Postcards

See if you can fit all your revision notes on a maximum number of, say, six plain postcards. Sorting and organising the information is excellent revision and, when you've made them, you can carry them around with you to take out and look at in a spare moment.

Audio

Why not tape yourself? Make up questions and leave spaces in which to answer. You could read the same thing over and over so that you brainwash yourself! Try a mixture of these. How about setting yourself a spelling test? The advantage is that you can listen back to yourself anywhere on a personal cassette or mini-disc player and shut out all distraction in the process.

Jigsaws

Get some postcards and put one fact or piece of information on each. Then cut each one in two, mix them all up and try putting them back together again!

If you're learning spellings, try matching cards with difficult spellings and their spelling rules.

Use pairs of cards to match up quotations and what they mean or suggest for the Shakespeare task.

EXAMINER'S TOP TIPS

Whatever type of revision suits your style of learning, do it. The more you identify areas of weakness and try to improve them, the higher you will go, regardless of your starting level.

When you have made a plan, stick to it. If you don't, you won't benefit!

Practice paper

In the following pages you will find:

A reading paper with short answer questions
A long writing task
A shorter writing task
A Shakespeare task

You will need paper on which to write your answers.

Reading paper

This paper contains three passages for you to read. You then need to answer the questions that follow.

You have **15 minutes** to read the three extracts.
You then have **one hour** to answer the questions that follow.
When you have answered the questions, check what you have written against the answers in the Answers section.

WEIRD SCIENCE!

Passage 1

Strange cars...

1 Designing cars is no easy task. Technology changes, tastes evolve and competition is fierce. Every year, major car manufacturers wheel out new models designed to dominate a given market and capture the attention of all consumers. Modern chassis give way to retro styling and accessories come and go. The whale boats of old, once considered stylish, become little old lady cars, and then, later still, classics coveted by the young and hip.

2 With all these variables in mind, it's easy to understand how some models emerge that are not quite like anything we've ever seen before. Here's the quirkiest car you'll notice on North American roads.

3 2004 Honda Insight
   Manufacturer's retail price: Between $19,180 & $21,380 US

4 Honda first introduced this gas-electric hybrid* in 1999. It's a two-seat hatchback that boasts the feel and experience of a regular car. In other words, Honda's aim was to sell it to you and me, not the guy who always buys the latest technology no matter what (remember Beta?).

5 The key selling point to this car is that, from the driver's perspective at least, it drives just like normal (no need to plug it in). A 67 horsepower engine may not sound like much, but this is a super lightweight car, tipping the scales at about 1,850 pounds. Combine this with fuel-efficient technology, and the Insight yields an amazing 66 miles to the gallon on the highway.

6 What makes it weird: From an aesthetic perspective, the Insight is a bit too revealing. Only a few drivers want everyone else on the road to know that they're driving a hybrid. The rest of us would probably be happy to drive hybrids if they looked the same, drove the same and cost less. Well, two out of three ain't bad for Honda's first hybrid market entry. But there's something about the design that makes you ask: Where's the rest of the car?

*hybrid – a mix of two different types of something, in this case, a mix of two different types of car (From www.askmen.com)

Passage 2
Invisible house

1 Think of how great it would be if you could just flick a switch and your house would become invisible. Now you can! Avoid solicitors, confuse unwanted guests, and never paint your house again. Be the first on your block to have an invisible house.

2 The principle is simple:

3 A matrix of large flat screen televisions, or monitors, covers the front of the house. Each of the flat screen monitors is connected to a video camera. Each camera is mounted on the rear interior wall of the house, facing outward through a small opening. This forms the 'video array' (Refer to Fig. 1a).

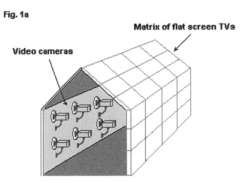

Fig. 1a

4 Signals from the 'video array' are sent to the flat screen monitors. An image of the backyard is thus displayed on the monitors, making the house invisible to anyone viewing it from the front (refer to Fig. 1b).

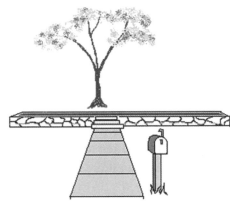

Matrix of flat screen TVs

Video cameras

5 Fine tuning is the key to good invisibility. Each monitor must have accurate color balance and synchronization. As well, each camera must be color balanced, synchronized, and aimed correctly.

Fig. 1b

Objects located behind house are displayed on front of house.

6 Note:
People who live in invisible houses should not throw stones! ...at least not at the house.

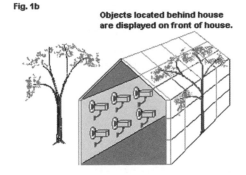

Passage 3

The time machine

1 The Time Traveller looked at us, and then at the mechanism. 'Well?' said the Psychologist.

2 'This little affair,' said the Time Traveller, resting his elbows upon the table and pressing his hands together above the apparatus, 'is only a model. It is my plan for a machine to travel through time. You will notice that it looks singularly askew, and that there is an odd twinkling appearance about this bar, as though it was in some way unreal.' He pointed to the part with his finger. 'Also, here is one little white lever, and here is another.'

3 The Medical Man got up out of his chair and peered into the thing. 'It's beautifully made,' he said.

4 'It took two years to make,' retorted the Time Traveller. Then, when we had all imitated the action of the Medical Man, he said: 'Now I want you clearly to understand that this lever, being pressed over, sends the machine gliding into the future, and this other reverses the motion. This saddle represents the seat of a time traveller. Presently I am going to press the lever, and off the machine will go. It will vanish, pass into future Time, and disappear. Have a good look at the thing. Look at the table too, and satisfy yourselves there is no trickery. I don't want to waste this model, and then be told I'm a quack.'

5 There was a minute's pause perhaps. The Psychologist seemed about to speak to me, but changed his mind. Then the Time Traveller put forth his finger towards the lever. 'No,' he said suddenly. 'Lend me your hand.' And turning to the Psychologist, he took that individual's hand in his own and told him to put out his forefinger. So that it was the Psychologist himself who sent forth the model Time Machine on its interminable voyage. We all saw the lever turn. I am absolutely certain there was no trickery. There was a breath of wind, and the lamp flame jumped. One of the candles on the mantel was blown out, and the little machine suddenly swung round, became indistinct, was seen as a ghost for a second perhaps, as an eddy of faintly glittering brass and ivory; and it was gone–vanished! Save for the lamp the table was bare.

6 Everyone was silent for a minute. Then Filby said he was damned.

7 The Psychologist recovered from his stupor, and suddenly looked under the table. At that the Time Traveller laughed cheerfully. 'Well?' he said, with a reminiscence of the Psychologist. Then, getting up, he went to the tobacco jar on the mantel, and with his back to us began to fill his pipe.

8 We stared at each other. 'Look here,' said the Medical Man, 'are you in earnest about this? Do you seriously believe that that machine has travelled into time?'

9 'Certainly,' said the Time Traveller, stooping to light a spill at the fire. Then he turned, lighting his pipe, to look at the Psychologist's face. (The Psychologist, to show that he was not unhinged, helped himself to a cigar and tried to light it uncut.) 'What is more, I have a big machine nearly finished in there'–he indicated the laboratory–'and when that is put together I mean to have a journey on my own account.'

From *The Time Machine* by HG Wells

Now answer the questions that follow.

1 From the first paragraph, give two reasons why designing cars is not easy. **(2 marks)**

2 a) In paragraph 1, why does the writer use the phrase 'wheel out'? **(1 mark)**

b) How does the phrase 'whale boats' make you feel dislike for old-fashioned cars? **(1 mark)**

3 a) The article is split into paragraphs with different topics. Complete this table by writing the correct paragraph number in the box next to the paragraph's topic. **(2marks)**

Topic	Paragraph number
Name and price of the car	
The background to the gas-electric car	
Overall summary of the car	
Linking from background to introduce the car	

b) Explain one reason why this text has personal comments as well as facts and technical language. **(1 mark)**

4 How does the article try to appeal to the type of people who might be interested in cars already? You should comment on the effect of:

The language used
The content of the article
The length of the paragraphs **(5 marks)**

5 a) From the first paragraph, write down one way that the writer tries to get the reader interested in his invention. **(1 mark)**

b) Why is a colon used after 'The principle is simple'? **(1 mark)**

6 How does the writer try to make the article seem serious? Choose two different words or phrases and explain how they create this effect on the reader. **(2 marks)**

Word/phrase	Effect on the reader	How it creates this effect on the reader
	makes the reader think that the article is serious	because it suggests
	makes the reader think that the article is serious	because it suggests

7 Which word in the first paragraph suggests that this was not written for a UK reader? **(1 mark)**

8 Why are inverted commas used around the phrase 'video array' in paragraph four? **(1 mark)**

9 In this article, how are language, grammar and content used to influence the reader? You should comment in your answer on the effect of the following:

The use of scientific words and phrases
Sentence lengths
The use of facts **(5 marks)**

Questions 10–13 are about the extract from 'The time machine' on page 84.

---

10 a) From this sentence – 'You will notice that it looks singularly askew, and that there is an odd twinkling appearance about this bar, as though it was in some way unreal' – write down one word that suggests the machine is mysterious. **(1 mark)**

b) Explain how this word creates a sense of mystery. **(1 mark)**

11 Explain why most of the characters have titles and not 'proper' names. **(2 marks)**

12 a) From the whole text, identify one feature of the Time Traveller's character. **(1 mark)**

b) From the whole text, identify one feature of the Psychologist's character. **(1 mark)**

13 a) Explain why paragraph six is so short. **(1 mark)**

b) What do you learn about the writer's viewpoint and purpose from the passage? Write down whether the following statements are true or false.
The writer wants to entertain the reader. True or false?
The writer is trying to give a serious scientific and factual study of time travel. True or false?
The writer is suggesting that nothing is impossible. True or false?
The writer is presenting science fiction as science fact. True or false? **(2 marks)**

The answers can be found in the Answers section at the back of this book.

Writing paper

This part of the test is one hour and 15 minutes long. It consists of the following:

Short writing task (20 marks, including 4 for spelling)
Long writing task (30 marks)

You should spend 30 minutes on the short writing task, including planning time.
You should spend 45 minutes on the long writing task, including planning time.

Writing paper – short writing task

(Spend 30 minutes on this.)

You write reviews for a school magazine. This week you have been asked to write a review of an MP3 music player.

Here is some information about the player:

> It is smaller than a pack of cards and weighs about the same.
>
> Its memory can hold 1000 songs.
>
> Its battery lasts for one hour and then needs to be recharged for two hours.
>
> It is extremely cheap – £10.
>
> Its sound quality is only average.

In your review, the school magazine editor wants you to:

analyse the features of the player
comment on what you thought about it.

Write your review of the MP3 music player.   **(20 marks, including 4 for spelling)**

The mark scheme can be found in the Answers section at the back of this book.

Writing paper – long writing task

Spend about 15 minutes planning your answer and 30 minutes writing.

Your local area, Palos Park, has been named as one of two areas where a multi-national company is looking to build a new factory building advanced computer parts.

You have been given the job of writing an article in your local newspaper to persuade the company to build in Palos Park and not the other location. Here are some facts about your area that you might wish to use.

The local college in Palos Park achieves some of the highest grades in technical subjects in the country.

The area has excellent transport links to the rest of the country.

There are large numbers of young people out of work in the area.

Workers in the area have never gone on strike.

The local council have just built a new, large housing estate.

Your newspaper editor wants you to write an article that:

- advises the company of the benefits of your area
- persuades them to build in Palos Park.

Write the article!   **(30 marks)**

The mark scheme can be found in the Answers section at the back of this book.

Shakespeare paper

This paper lasts 45 minutes. It is worth 18 marks.

In the SATs you will do a question based on set scenes in the play you are studying. This question has been designed so that you can create your own task, based on the scenes you are studying this year.

The question will expect you to look at parts of two scenes. You will examine a feature, for example a character, from one scene and then look at that same feature in your other scene. You may be asked how that feature or character has changed in the second of your two scenes.

Pick a character from the first scene you are studying – it needs to be a character that appears in your second scene too. Then attempt this question.

You should spend 45 minutes on this section.

Shakespeare scenes

In your two scenes, your chosen character changes.

How does your character change and how does Shakespeare show these changes?

Support your ideas by referring to both of the scenes you have been told to study by your English teacher.

(18 marks)

The mark scheme can be found in the Answers section at the back of this book.

Glossary

Accent – the way that someone pronounces words, as a result of their location or social class

Adjectives – words that describe nouns

Adverbs – words that describe how you do things; they describe verbs

Alliteration – words close together starting with the same letter or sound

Composition and effect – in the SATs mark scheme, this section earns you marks for writing in a suitable style

Conditional phrases – phrases that use words like 'could' or 'might'

Connectives – words or phrases that link sentences or paragraphs

Context – the setting of the writing

Emotive language – words that are used on purpose to make you feel certain emotions

Enjambment – in poetry, where one line continues onto another

Figurative language – words or phrases that have deeper layers of meaning

Formal – something, e.g. writing, that is done in a generally accepted way

Imperative verbs – verbs that act as commands or instructions, usually found at the start of a sentence

Informal – something, e.g. writing, that is done in a way that is generally not accepted

Main clause – a clause that contains a subject and a verb and stands alone as a complete sentence

Metaphor – a comparison, where one thing is said to be another

Modal verbs – verbs like 'could', 'should' or 'might' used in conditional phrases

Monologue – a story told by one person to an audience or reader

Onomatopoeia – words that sound like the thing they are describing

Question focus – the main point of what the question is about

Reassuring vocabulary – words that make you feel safe

Repetition – words that occur several times, for a particular effect

Rhetorical question – one that implies or suggests an answer, but doesn't give it

Sequential – in order, or sequence

Simile – a comparison that uses 'as' or 'like'

Specialist audience – a set of readers who are interested in the same topic

Subordinate clause – a phrase that adds extra information to the main purpose of the sentence

Systematic – one step at a time

Third person viewpoint – spoken by a narrator

Three-part repetition – a technique used in persuasive writing or speech that works by making the listener or reader think they have a good deal

Tone – the mood of a piece of writing

Topic sentences – found at or near the start of paragraphs, they contain the main idea of that paragraph

Answers

In this section, you will find the answers to the revision sections and the mark schemes for the practice paper.

Test your knowledge 1

1 You can have these in any order. Give yourself 1 mark for each correct one.

1. Argue 2. Persuade 3. Advise 4. Inform 5. Explain 6. Describe 7. Explore 8. Imagine 9. Entertain 10. Analyse 11. Review 12. Comment

2 Give yourself 1 mark for each correct answer.

a) Use flattery – Persuade, possibly Argue
b) Look at two sides of an issue – Argue, possibly Persuade
c) Use formal language – Any of the 12 types, depending on the task
d) Use similes and metaphors – Explore, Imagine Entertain mainly
e) Give personal opinions – Argue, Persuade, Advise mainly
f) Use informal language – Any of the 12 types, depending on the task
g) Use facts and statistics – Argue, Persuade, Advise, Inform, Explain, Describe, Analyse, Review, Comment

3 For each example, give yourself 1 mark for the writing type and up to 3 marks for identifying the features.

Example 1 – Writing to Argue: It contains facts and opinions. It looks at two sides of an issue. It uses rhetorical questions.

Example 2 – Writing to Persuade: It uses flattery, guilt, reassurance, rhetorical questions and three-part repetition.

Example 3 – Writing to Explore, Imagine and Entertain: It contains adjectives, similes, alliteration and metaphors.

Example 4 – Writing to Inform, Explain and Describe: It is written in an ordered sequence, it contains facts and statistics, and personal comment.

Test your knowledge 2

1 Give yourself 1 mark for each correct answer.

a) It can be written in the third person – all three
b) It can be written in the first person – all three
c) It can contain similes, metaphors, alliteration or onomatopoeia – all three
d) It can be written with a narrator who talks directly to the audience/reader – all three
e) It can contain speech – all three

2 Give yourself 1 mark for each correct answer.

a) rhetorical question
b) hyperbole
c) euphemism
d) onomatopoeia
e) parody
f) ellipsis
g) alliteration
h) metaphor
i) personification
j) simile

3 The only technique not used in the passage is parody. (1 mark)

4 Give yourself 1 mark for each correct answer.

a) delightful
b) temperate
c) calm
d) miffed
e) sauntering

Test your knowledge 3

1 Give yourself 1 mark for each correct answer. The most likely combinations are as follows:

a) Information, Recount, Explanation, Instructions, Review
b) Explanation, Instructions, Persuasion, Review, Editorial/Opinion
c) Persuasion, Review, Editorial/Opinion, Description
d) Instructions
e) Description
f) Information, Recount, Explanation, Instructions, Persuasion, Review, Editorial/Opinion
g) Information, Recount, Persuasion, Review, Editorial/Opinion, Description
h) Information, Recount, Explanation, Instructions, Persuasion, Review, Editorial/ Opinion

2 For each paragraph, give yourself 1 mark for the text type and 1 mark for each reason, to a maximum of 3.

Paragraph 1 is Review writing – it contains personal opinion, it uses technical words to do with film and music and has an overall verdict.

Paragraph 2 is Instruction writing – sentences begin with imperative verbs, it is in a sequenced order and sentences are short.

Paragraph 3 is Description writing – it contains personal opinion, uses adjectives and adverbs and has an informal personal tone.

Paragraph 4 is Editorial/Opinion writing – it contains rhetorical questions, gives biased opinions and has a clear conclusion, which states a strong opinion.

Practice paper

Reading paper – short answer questions

1 1 mark for each of the following, up to a maximum of 2: Technology changes/Tastes evolve/Competition is fierce/New models are brought out/Fashions change

2 a) Because it is a motoring pun   (1 mark)
   b) It suggests that the old cars were big and clumsy
                               (1 mark)

3 a) Name and price of car – Paragraph 3
     The background of the gas-electric car – Paragraph 1
     Overall summary of the car – Paragraph 6
     Linking from background to introduce the car – Paragraph 2
     (0–1 right = 0 marks; 2–3 right = 1 mark; 4 right = 2 marks)
   b) They are two methods of persuading the reader of the car's merit.

4 Simple points made about the article, with limited awareness of how the writer tries to appeal to people.   (1 mark)

Two examples of how the article is trying to appeal to people, with some comment on how the text has this effect. Some awareness of effect is evident. Two of the three bullet points are addressed briefly.   (2 marks)

Shows some understanding of how content is used to make the article appeal to people and aware of how the language and paragraph lengths affect the reader. Some references to the text are included to support ideas. The third bullet point is only briefly addressed.   (3 marks)

Some exploration of how the text tries to affect the reader though all three bullet points. A consistent attempt to comment on all three bullet points. References are used appropriately to support all ideas.   (4 marks)

A focused response that explores in detail how the article affects the reader, with close, precise reference to the text, picking out individual words and phrases. All three bullet points are addressed and a high level of awareness is shown by an understanding of different techniques that the writer has used.   (5 marks)

5 a) 1 mark for either of the following: It makes the experience seem unique. It appeals to people who like to be first.
   b) To introduce an explanation   (1 mark)

6 1 mark for each example plus explanation, up to a maximum of 2. No marks for explanation without an example, or an example without an explanation.

7 The word 'block'   (1 mark)

8 Inverted commas are used because the phrase has been invented by the writer.   (1 mark)

9 Simple points made about the article, with limited awareness of how the writer tries to influence people.   (1 mark)

Two examples of how the article is trying to influence people, with some comment on how the text has this effect. Some awareness of effect is evident. Two of the three bullet points are addressed briefly.   (2 marks)

Shows some understanding of how facts are used to make the article appeal to people and aware of how the language and sentence lengths affect the reader. Some references to the text are included to support ideas. The third bullet point is only briefly addressed.   (3 marks)

Some exploration of how the text tries to affect the reader though all three bullet points. A consistent attempt to comment on all three bullet points. References are used appropriately to support all ideas.   (4 marks)

A focused response that explores in detail how the article affects the reader, with close, precise reference to the text, picking out individual words and phrases. All three bullet points are addressed and a high level of awareness is shown by an understanding of different techniques that the writer has used.   (5 marks)

10 a) 1 mark maximum for any of the following: singularly/odd/unreal
    b) 1 mark for any valid explanation

11 Because the writer wants us to see how they represent different views on time travel.   (1 mark)

12 a) 1 mark maximum for any of the following: he is methodical/likes to shock people/intelligent/open minded

   b) 1 mark maximum for either of the following: doubting/curious

13 a) It is short because the writer wants to create a feeling of tension   (1 mark)

   b) The writer wants to entertain the reader. True

   The writer is trying to give a serious scientific and factual study of time travel. False

   The writer is suggesting that nothing is impossible. True

   The writer is presenting science fiction as science fact. True

   (0–1 right = 0 marks; 2–3 right = 1 mark; 4 right = 2 marks)

Mark schemes

The bands for writing give descriptions of the main features to look out for in your writing. Different bands have different amounts of marks in them.

For bands with three different marks, check the following.

- If your writing fits everything in that band, but shows no evidence of the bands above or below, give yourself the middle mark.
- If your writing fits everything in that band, but shows one piece of evidence of lower bands, give yourself the lower mark in the band.
- If your writing fits everything in that band, but shows one piece of evidence of higher bands, give yourself the higher mark in the band.

For bands with two marks, you need to do two of the things in the band to get the lower mark and everything in the band to get the higher mark.

For bands with one mark, you need to do everything in that band to get that mark.

Long writing task – mark scheme for all papers

Section A: Sentence structure and punctuation

Band A1
- Sentences and phrases are mostly linked with joining words like 'and', 'but' and 'when'.
- Sentences are simple and may contain lots of repeated words and phrases.
- Full stops, capital letters and exclamation marks are used to punctuate sentences, mostly accurately.
                                        (0 marks)

Band A2
- Sentences are varied and more complex joining words like 'who' and 'which' are used.
- Words like 'if' and 'because' are used to help give reasons and for emphasising ideas.
- Commas are used quite accurately within sentences.
                                        (1 or 2 marks)

Band A3
- Simple and more complex sentences are used – long sentences and short sentences are used successfully.
- Suggestions are given, by using words like 'can' or 'would'.
- A variety of punctuation is used with accuracy.
- Different types of sentences, e.g. commands, questions or exclamations, are used in order to create more interesting effects.
                                        (3 or 4 marks)

Band A4
- The writer begins sentences more skilfully, with words like 'usually' or 'hopefully' etc. or by being impersonal, e.g. 'Some people believe that...'
- A range of punctuation is used and this is sometimes done for deliberate effect, e.g. brackets are used to put in asides and thoughts.
                                        (5 or 6 marks)

Band A5
- Sentences are varied depending on the effect that the writer wishes to create.
- Simple sentences might be used, but to create effects, e.g. shock or surprise.
- Punctuation is used skilfully in order to make the reader speed up and slow down, and to make the meaning of the writing perfectly clear.
                                        (7 marks)

Band A6
- A wide range of sentence types is used with skill, accuracy and thought to control the writing.
- There might be some non-standard sentences, but used for deliberate effect.
- There is a very wide range of different types of punctuation used, in order to create a number of different effects.
                                        (8 marks)

Section B: Text structure and organisation

This section focuses on how overall meaning and effect is put across through the way that the writing is organised and planned.

Band B1
- Ideas are mainly linked because they happen to be on the same topic.
- Points might be put in a list, but not necessarily in any sort of order of importance.

- Paragraphs might be used to show some of the obvious different topics in the writing.

(0 marks)

Band B2
- Paragraphs usually start with the main topic in the first sentence.
- The paragraphs will contain examples.
- The letter has some brief opening and closing comments, but they will be fairly brief and undeveloped.

(1 or 2 marks)

Band B3
- Paragraphs are written in a logical order.
- The introduction and conclusion are clear.
- Paragraphs of different lengths are used, e.g. short paragraphs might take the form of a persuasive question.

(3 or 4 marks)

Band B4
- Detailed content is well handled within and between paragraphs.
- Some phrases like 'On the other hand' or 'In addition to this' etc. are used to link the paragraphs.
- The introduction and conclusion to the letter are developed and help to make it more persuasive.

(5 or 6 marks)

Band B5
- Paragraphs are varied in length to suit the different ideas being discussed.
- The paragraphs are linked with a variety of words and phrases.
- Paragraphs are ordered in such a way that the writer might have used them to highlight contrasts, or to be ironic.

(7 marks)

Band B6
- The whole piece of writing is organised, shaped and controlled to achieve a range of effects, or to get the reader thinking in a certain way.
- Within paragraphs, the writer has used a wide range of links that are precisely and carefully chosen.

(8 marks)

Section C: Composition and effect

This section focuses on the overall impact on the writing and the effect it has on the reader.

Band C1
- The writing shows some awareness of the reader.
- There is some relevant content.

(0 marks)

Band C2
- The writing is generally lively and attempts to interest the reader.
- The content of the writing shows that the writer recognises its purpose.
- Some reasons are given for the ideas and opinions, but perhaps not that many.

(1, 2 or 3 marks)

Band C3
- The writing is detailed and gives clear reasons for the opinions and viewpoints expressed.
- The writing engages the reader's interest.
- The writing gives a range of relevant ideas and the writer's viewpoint is clear.

(4, 5 or 6 marks)

Band C4
- The piece is well written because it uses a range of techniques such as repetition, humour and a consideration of the reader's needs in order to persuade.
- The writer's view is consistent.

(7, 8 or 9 marks)

Band C5
- The tone and content of the writing are appropriate and well judged.
- The writing deliberately interacts with the reader.
- Content is relevant throughout and is used to support the ideas.

(10, 11 or 12 marks)

Band C6
- The writing has been done skilfully and the writer is totally in control of the writing type.
- The viewpoint of the writer has been maintained throughout.
- There is a strong individual style, created by a range of methods.

(13 or 14 marks)

Short writing task – mark scheme for all papers

Section D: Sentence structure/punctuation and paragraph organisation

This section focuses on how you choose to organise your writing and how this contributes to its overall effect.

Band D1
- Sentences are fairly simple.
- Sentences are linked by simple joining words like 'and' or 'then'.
- Full stops and capital letters are used with accuracy.
- Paragraphs are used to separate the more obvious different topics given in the task.

(0 marks)

Band D2
- Sentences are varied and use linking words like 'who' or 'which'.
- The writing is written in the same tense throughout.
- Words like 'he', 'she', 'it', 'they' and other pronouns are generally used correctly
- Paragraphs are mainly put into a logical order, as is the detail within them.

(1 or 2 marks)

Band D3
- A variety of longer sentences is used. This includes those that have been built up from joining simpler ones together to make longer ones and sentences where the word order has been successfully rearranged for effect.
- Words like 'completely', 'partly' and others, which help to make meaning more precise, are used.
- Words like 'he', 'she', 'it', 'they' and other pronouns are used correctly.
- Tenses are used correctly.
- Paragraphs are used for appropriate reasons and are put into a logical order.
- The detail in them is put into a logical order.

(3 or 4 marks)

Band D4
- Sentences are written in a variety of ways to achieve interesting effects that suit the purpose of the writing.
- A range of punctuation is used – sometimes to create effects.
- Paragraphs are of different lengths and the information in them is organised cleverly to suit what is being written about.

(5 marks)

Band D5
- There is a wide range of sentence structures that use a sophisticated range of verbs and tenses.
- Within paragraphs, the writer has used a wide range of links that are precisely and carefully chosen.
- There is a very wide range of punctuation used in order to make meaning clear and create a range of effects.

(6 marks)

Section E: Composition and effect

This section is to do with the overall impact of your writing and how well it fits the audience you are writing for.

Band E1
- The writing shows some awareness of the reader.
- Simple techniques, like repetition, are used.
- Content is relevant to the question, but might well be unevenly used.

(0 marks)

Band E2
- The writing tries to interest the reader.
- Some techniques, e.g. use of adjectives, are used to help writing, but they might not be very imaginative.

(1, 2 or 3 marks)

Band E3
- The writer interests the reader.
- The writer is clearly aware of what type of writing he/she is doing and for whom.
- The tone of the writing is consistent throughout.

(4, 5 or 6 marks)

Band E4
- The writing is well written and convincing throughout.
- The writer really engages the reader's interest.
- There is a very good range of well-chosen details.
- The viewpoint of the writer is consistent throughout.

(7, 8 or 9 marks)

Band E5
- The writing has been done skilfully and the writer is totally in control of the writing type.
- The viewpoint of the writer has been maintained throughout.
- There is a strong individual style, created by a range of methods.

(10 marks)

Section F: Spelling
This section focuses on accuracy in spelling. Choose the section that best fits the writing.

Band F1
- Simple words and those with more than one or two syllables are generally accurate.

(1 mark)

Band F2
- More complicated words that fit to regular patterns and rules are generally accurate.

(2 marks)

Band F3
- Most spelling, including irregular words, is accurate.

(3 marks)

Band F4
- Virtually all spelling, including complex words that don't fit to regular rules or patterns, is correct.

(4 marks)

Shakespeare question – mark scheme

The mark bands apply to all Shakespeare questions.

Find the band that best fits your answer and for every bullet point in that band that you achieve, give yourself 1 mark within that band. So, if you think you are in Band 4 and you have done two of the bullet points, then you should give yourself 11.

Band 1
- A few simple facts and opinions about these extracts.
- There may be some misunderstandings.
- Parts of the extracts are retold or copied and answers may be only partly relevant.

(1, 2 or 3 marks)

Band 2
- Contains a little explanation, showing some awareness of the needs of the question.
- Comments are relevant but are mostly about the plot.
- Some broad references to how the character speaks.

(4, 5 or 6 marks)

Band 3
- Some general understanding of the question, although some points might not be developed.
- Some comments on the language that the character uses.
- Some points backed up with reference to the text.

(7, 8 or 9 marks)

Band 4
- Some discussion of how the extracts relate to the question, even though all the ideas might not be of equal quality.
- Awareness of the character's use of language and its effects
- Most points backed up with references to the text.

(10, 11 or 12 marks)

Band 5
- Clear focus on how the extracts relate to the question.
- Good consistent comments on the character's language and its effects.
- Well-chosen quotations linked together to present an overall argument.

(13, 14 or 15 marks)

Band 6
- Every quotation is analysed in depth with relation to the question.
- Every quotation is commented on in terms of the language that the character uses.
- Individual words are picked out of quotations and linked into the overall argument.

(16, 17 or 18 marks)